D1267244

The Enduring Reagan

The Enduring Reagan

Edited by
Charles W. Dunn

THE UNIVERSITY PRESS OF KENTUCKY

Scholarly publisher for the Commonwealth,
serving Bellarmine University, Berea College, Centre College of Kentucky,
Eastern Kentucky University, The Filson Historical Society, Georgetown
College, Kentucky Historical Society, Kentucky State University,
Morehead State University, Murray State University, Northern Kentucky
University, Transylvania University, University of Kentucky, University of
Louisville, and Western Kentucky University.
All rights reserved.

Editorial and Sales Offices: The University Press of Kentucky
663 South Limestone Street, Lexington, Kentucky 40508-4008
www.kentuckypress.com

13 12 11 10 09   5 4 3 2 1

Library of Congress Cataloging-in-Publication Data

The enduring Reagan / edited by Charles W. Dunn.
    p. cm.
    Includes bibliographical references and index.
    ISBN 978-0-8131-2552-7 (hardcover : alk. paper)
    1. Reagan, Ronald. 2. Reagan, Ronald—Political and social views.
3. Reagan, Ronald—Influence. 4. Presidents—United States—Biography.
5. Conservatism—United States—History—20th century. 6. United States—
Politics and government—1981-1989. I. Dunn, Charles W.
    E877.E78 2009
    973.927092—dc22
    [B]   2009018230

This book is printed on acid-free recycled paper meeting
the requirements of the American National Standard
for Permanence in Paper for Printed Library Materials.

Manufactured in the United States of America.

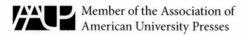 Member of the Association of
American University Presses

CONTENTS

Introduction

THE IRONY OF RONALD REAGAN

Charles W. Dunn

> History is replete with proofs, from Cato the Elder to Kennedy the Younger, that if you scratch a statesman you will find an actor, but it is becoming harder and harder in our day, to tell government from show business.
>
> —James Thurber

Critics contended that Ronald Reagan was nothing more than a third-rate Hollywood actor who lacked sufficient intellectual depth and educational training to serve successfully as president. Coming from the small town of Dixon in the midst of flat Illinois cornfields, raised by a very religious mother, Nelle, whose training led him to become a Sunday school teacher of grade-school boys, a graduate of a tiny and little-known religious college, Eureka, Reagan hardly had the pedigree to become president of the United States in the late twentieth century. But he defied that and more to confound the critics. So how did Reagan beat the odds? That which discounted and discredited his potential laid the foundation for his prominence.

IRONY 1: COUNTERINTUITIVE BACKGROUND

The foundation for Reagan's reputation as the "Great Communicator" was laid during his boyhood.[1] In midwestern Protestant churches of that era, Sunday school and church played prominent roles in child

1

rearing. Growing up in that environment under his mother's strict tutelage, Reagan learned the discipline of weekly Sunday school and church attendance, heard the mesmerizing stories of Bible heroes, sat under countless and usually long sermons, and listened to the exciting stories of missionaries in faraway places. He attended Sunday school and church on Sunday morning, Christian Endeavor and church again on Sunday night, and prayer meeting on Wednesday night. Except in cold weather, his mother and he walked the seven blocks to church. But it didn't stop there. They also attended special church services and other religious events. And in the home, his mother featured daily Bible reading and prayer.

Oral communication, recitations, and performances in plays were part of that environment. Reagan took to this environment, memorizing and reciting various readings, performing in plays, and traveling to other churches to do the same, earning at a young age a reputation for excellence in communication. And then, at the age of fifteen, he began to teach a boys' Sunday school class, which gained a reputation for no discipline problems because of Reagan's captivating communication skills. Even after he left for Eureka College, 108 miles away, he returned to teach his Sunday school class. Years later, while serving as governor of California, Reagan wrote to his boyhood pastor, Ben Cleaver, "One thing I do know, all the hours in the old church in Dixon . . . and all of Nelle's faith have come together in a kind of inheritance without which I'd be lost and helpless."

His two favorite books from childhood were the Bible and *That Printer of Udell's: A Story of the Middle West* (1903), which told of the son of a drunken father, whose excellent speaking ability helped him to become a successful preacher. Central to the book was the theme that God has a plan for everyone. Reagan saw himself as a person of divine destiny. In 1968, as the governor of California, he commented, "I'm not quite able to explain how my election happened or why I'm here, apart from believing it is part of God's plan for me."

Without his boyhood training, Reagan could hardly have earned his enduring reputation as the Great Communicator, nor would he have developed the accompanying character traits of courage, discipline, and vision. Combined, they became the launching pad for his rise to prominence.

IRONY 2: COUNTERINTUITIVE DECISIONS

Swimming upstream against the downstream current of popular thinking sometimes constitutes the best test of a person's character. Only a fine line may separate courage and folly when one swims upstream, but Reagan's decisions usually fell on the courageous side of that fine line. He had a knack for doing the unexpectedly courageous and what many, including his closest advisers, thought to be unwise. In short, Ronald Reagan defied common wisdom. In stock-market parlance, his investments in high-risk stocks paid high dividends. And as an investor, he stayed with his investments over the long haul.

Reagan's first venture on departing from Eureka College and Dixon, Illinois, but before leaving the Midwest for California, was as a sports announcer on the newly emerging medium of radio in Des Moines, Iowa. His job: to deliver play-by-play accounts of games as though he were there, based on telegraph reports. Reagan's fertile imagination translated plain telegraph copy into exciting oral imagery over the radio airwaves to unseen audiences, further perfecting his communication skills. After that, his much better known acting career in Hollywood began, which propelled him to the position of president of the Screen Actors Guild. In that position he began his forays into politics as a member of the Democratic Party and as an archenemy of Communist influence in the Hollywood acting community. Gradually during the 1950s, as a popular speaker for General Electric, he refined his political beliefs as an anti-Communist and as a proponent of free-market economics and traditional social values, which set the stage for a sequence of decisions.

- In 1962, just two years before the Republican Party hit rock bottom during Barry Goldwater's landslide loss for the presidency, Reagan switched parties. In doing so, he became one of the first neoconservatives, ardent Democrats who identified with Franklin D. Roosevelt and the New Deal but who became disenchanted with what they perceived as their party's leftward drift in foreign affairs and undue expansion of social welfare policies.

- In 1964 Reagan became the principal speaker for Senator Goldwater's presidential campaign, despite the widespread anticipation that Goldwater would suffer one of the worst defeats in presidential campaign history. Goldwater won just six states: five in the old South and his home state, Arizona.

- In 1966 Reagan twice challenged the oddsmakers: first by beating the popular mayor of San Francisco, Warren Christopher, for the Republican gubernatorial nomination, and then by beating the popular incumbent governor of California, Edmund "Pat" Brown.

- In 1968 he briefly flirted with a challenge to Richard Nixon's campaign for the Republican presidential nomination.

- In 1975, after serving eight years as governor of California, Reagan launched a nationwide radio program, which most of his advisers opposed because they wanted him to concentrate on television. The payoff was dramatic. His 1,027 radio commentaries, which touted his conservative ideas while flying under the radar of television, reached some 20 to 30 million listeners weekly between 1975 and 1979.

- In 1976, he narrowly lost a close race for the Republican presidential nomination against an incumbent president, Gerald R. Ford, who had all the power of the White House at his disposal.

- In 1980, running as the Republican nominee for president against the one-term Democratic president Jimmy Carter, Reagan won a landslide victory. How significant was that? Only once since the Civil War had a one-term president lost a race for reelection—Grover Cleveland in 1888.

As president, Reagan pursued policies that often conflicted with normative thought. Economically he advocated supply-side economics in the form of the Laffer curve, named after the economist Arthur Laffer. In many circles the Laffer curve was laughable, because it counterintuitively contended that decreases in taxes would not only spark economic growth but also increase government revenues. In building a majority congressional coalition in support of supply-side economics, Reagan won converts to the Republican Party, such as U.S. representative and later senator Phil Gramm of Texas.

In foreign policy, Reagan's air-strike interventions in Grenada and Libya drew opposition, but they worked, preventing a Communist takeover in the former and forcing the latter to back away from its expansionist policies. However, far beyond these in significance were his decisions to build up the American military as a challenge to the Soviet Union and then to proclaim, "Mr. Gorbachev, tear down this wall." Both directly defied America's reigning orthodox foreign and military policy based on the cold war idea of containment. Soon after Reagan's challenges, the Berlin Wall toppled, and Communists tumbled from power in the Soviet Union and its satellite states in Central and Eastern Europe.

Irony 3: Counterintuitive Expectations

Ironically a low bar of expectations benefited Ronald Reagan. Political analysts know that having a low bar of expectations and exceeding it is far better than having a high bar and either failing to exceed it or only barely doing so. Because critics underestimated Reagan's abilities, they set a low bar of expectations, which he consistently exceeded. For example, his popular image as an actor belied his personal behavior as a hard worker and a well-read person. His 1,027 radio commentaries between 1975 and 1979 illustrate this paradox.[2]

First, to what extent did Reagan do the work? The texts of 670 commentaries were in his own handwriting, and some of the remaining were written by him, but his handwritten text cannot be found. The rest were written by staff members. Another 9, though written by him, were apparently never delivered.

Second, what did he address in these commentaries? Economic issues, including regulatory policies, taxation, government spending, employment, and monetary policy; environmental and energy issues; and social issues, including welfare, education, Social Security, national health insurance, and Medicare.

Third, what do the commentaries reveal about Reagan's reading habits? He cited and quoted a variety of publications, such as *Commentary,* the *National Review, Human Events,* the *American Spectator,* the *New York Times,* and the *Wall Street Journal.* And books that he was reading also made their way into his commentaries.

Contrary to appearances, Reagan's conservatism was pragmatic. To borrow a religious term, he was ecumenical in his efforts to unify economic, political, religious, and social conservatism. And as though he were a chemist, he devised a formula for mixing them with just the right amount of each: the free-market ideas of economic conservatives, the emphasis on freedom and liberty of political conservatives, the importance of orthodox moral and religious beliefs of religious conservatives, and the respect for order and tradition of social conservatives. He blended enough of each to win the Republican nomination against George H. W. Bush, and then, during the general campaign and his presidency, he moved enough to the center to win and govern. Also knowing that conservatives in foreign policy have two wings—interventionist and isolationist—he walked on the balance beam between them, using the language of both internationalism and nationalism as needed.

Conservatives often have a command-and-control style of leadership and a reputation for being hard-nosed. Reagan was neither. As president he had an indirect leadership style, laying out broad ideological principles and entrusting his subordinates to carry them out. In that he was like an impressionist painter whose bold brushstrokes created on the canvas of politics and public policy his desired image and direction. Administratively his style was a blend of Franklin D. Roosevelt and Dwight D. Eisenhower, the opposite of Richard Nixon and Jimmy Carter, who absorbed themselves in the details of governing.

As a former governor, like Jimmy Carter, without experience in Washington DC, and as a conservative facing what conservatives deemed to be a city dominated by liberals, Reagan might have been expected to govern as an outsider, as Carter did. Instead he cultivated close relationships with the Washington establishment, particularly with congressional Democrats, who had long controlled Congress. When appropriate, he used his national popularity as an outsider to gain influence as an insider.

Rather than being hard-nosed, Reagan was given to compromise on key issues. He understood the limits of ideology in American politics—that to get things done he must compromise, share, and sometimes give the credit to others, including his political foes. He recognized that Americans' political beliefs resemble a bell curve. Most are neither conservative nor liberal but centrist. And so a successful politician must appeal to the middle. Reagan never jettisoned his conservative ideology, but he knew that to succeed he must appeal to the center. Put another

way, because he saw his conservative ideology not as the meat and pota-
toes of politics but as the seasoning, he sprinkled conservative seasoning
on the center of American politics.

As a candidate for president in 1980, he advocated abolishing the
U.S. Department of Education, but as president he did not push for its
abolition because of insufficient support in Congress. Lacking a governing majority, he had to set priorities to advance portions of his agenda,
which at times alienated some of his followers, especially religious and
social conservatives, who thought that as president he no longer took
as staunch a position on abortion and other social issues as he had as a
candidate.

In an age of policy wonks, Reagan was the antiwonk. He relied on a
few principles to guide his thinking on politics and public policy. These
principles were like a grid that he used to determine his positions on
issues. Refusing to get bogged down in interminable debates about the
minutiae of politics and policy, he chose to advocate broad, general
principles that the American people could understand.

Frequently critics inveighed against his simplistic, moral language
and his seeming aloofness from the details of policy. In both instances,
they mistook him. His seemingly simplistic, moral language spoke to the
heart of Americans, who liked such phrases as "It's morning in America." And he further lifted the public spirit by referring to America as "a
shining city upon a hill," quoting John Winthrop. By lifting the American spirit, Reagan was able to get Americans behind his initiatives. Numerous times his televised Oval Office chats with the American people
caused them to flood the Capitol switchboard the next day on behalf of
his policy positions. In an era of relativism, he spoke of moral absolutes,
even testifying to his personal faith in Jesus Christ as his Savior and to
his belief in the Genesis account of creation, positions he had held since
childhood, which contributed to his strong support from the emerging
evangelical voting bloc.

Believing that individuals could make a difference in the flow of history, Reagan did not see history as moving inevitably in one direction.
When Reagan began to take conservative ideology seriously during the
1950s, he did so against a backdrop of overwhelming liberal ascendancy
and supremacy in politics. As one of America's leading thinkers, Lionel
Trilling, put it in 1950, "In the United States at this time, liberalism is
not only the dominant but even the sole intellectual tradition. For it is

the plain fact that nowadays there are no conservative . . . ideas in general circulation."[3]

Trilling was right. There were no conservative ideas in general circulation. But there was a latent reservoir of conservative intellectual thought. A variety of conservative thinkers had hammered out a wide-ranging conservative philosophy, including such monumental works as Richard Weaver's *Ideas Have Consequences* (1948), Peter Viereck's *Conservatism Revisited* (1949), William F. Buckley's *God and Man at Yale* (1951), Russell Kirk's *The Conservative Mind* (1953), Whittaker Chambers's *Witness* (1953), and Clinton Rossiter's *Conservatism in America* (1955). What they needed was someone who understood their philosophy and who could communicate it to the popular audience. That was where Ronald Reagan came in. He was the bridge between philosophical and popular conservatism.

Reagan was more than that, however. He understood that conservatism needed a new face, that of the "Happy Warrior." Someone different from Senator Barry Goldwater, whose popular *Conscience of a Conservative* (1961) galvanized some, but not all, strands of conservatism. Goldwater's stern rhetoric, as illustrated by his most famous, some say infamous, line delivered at the 1964 Republican National Convention in San Francisco—"Extremism in the defense of liberty is no vice. . . . Moderation in the pursuit of justice is no virtue"—struck Americans, including many conservatives, negatively. Reagan's rhetoric and ecumenical spirit enabled him to become conservatism's Happy Warrior.

Ironically Reagan used nonconservative means to advance his conservative agenda. Historically conservatives have opposed the expansion of executive power, especially beginning with Franklin D. Roosevelt and continuing through Lyndon B. Johnson. Reagan not only used these expanded powers handed down to him by liberal Democrats but also expanded them himself.

In many quarters, especially in university life, conservatives are perceived as anti-intellectual, and, of course, Reagan suffered from an image of anti-intellectualism. In truth, not only did his wide-ranging reading habits contradict this perception, but his array of intellectual presidential advisers also belied this notion. He probably encircled himself with as many intellectual advisers as had any president from Roosevelt through Johnson, including John F. Kennedy.

Academics have long had a love affair with such activist presidents as Franklin D. Roosevelt, believing that they are necessary to implement a progressive agenda and to counter a sluggish Congress. Academics thought Reagan would be a passive president, more in the mold of Eisenhower, but he surprised them. Reagan was an activist, but not on behalf of academics' aspirations. Reagan led Congress and the nation in bold, new, conservative directions.

The ultimate counterintuitive expectation was simply this: Reagan confounded his critics and exceeded the low bar of expectations set for him. Critics complained then that Reagan had a Teflon coating that kept criticisms and failures from sticking to him. Why? We do not rightly know. Maybe it's difficult for criticisms and failures to stick to a person of whom less is expected. Regardless, one thing is certain: history has once again confounded the critics. Reagan's Teflon coating is more durable today than it was then.

Irony 4: Counterintuitive History

"And they said it couldn't be done." Not only was it done, but now, more than twenty years since the end of his presidency, Reagan's successes loom larger as his failures fade, much to the chagrin of his critics. Reagan had several shortcomings, including his record on civil rights, the Iran-contra flap, and judicial nominations. Strangely, however, his failures sometimes laid the groundwork for success, as was the case with his judicial nominations. What he called for later happened, largely because of the vanguard of young conservatives he inspired to enter politics. They, following after, fought for his ideas. And many now occupy positions on the U.S. Supreme Court and throughout the federal judiciary.

What was Reagan like? Some might say that he embodied the virtues of many presidents.

- Like Roosevelt, he was bold and daring.
- Like Truman, he exceeded his critics' expectations.
- Like Eisenhower, he gave Americans a sense of peace and tranquility.
- Like Kennedy, he motivated with a sterling command of language.
- Like Johnson, he expanded the powers of the presidency.
- Like Nixon, he pursued an activist conservative agenda.

- Like Ford, he worked well with his political adversaries.
- Like Carter, he brought a sense of the sacred to the Oval Office.

We should never forget the irony that without Carter, who became only the second one-term president since the Civil War to lose his re-election campaign, there would have been no Reagan. Carter's failures, including his depressing emphasis on "malaise" in America, set the stage for Reagan's successes and his cheerful optimism: "It's morning in America."

The greatest presidents forge new pathways of thinking and achieve successes that force their successors to govern within the confines of their legacy. Stephen Skowronek refers to them as creators of a "new orthodoxy" in public policy.[4] Such was Ronald Wilson Reagan. Like a giant ocean liner, he left a wake behind him that circumscribed the movements of his successors, George H. W. Bush, Bill Clinton, and George W. Bush. Few presidents leave such a legacy. George Washington, Thomas Jefferson, Andrew Jackson, Abraham Lincoln, Franklin D. Roosevelt, and Ronald Reagan did.

"Where is Ronald Reagan when we need him?" That is the cry of today's conservatives and the Republican Party, who have lost their way in the forest of American politics by putting politics above principle, partisanship above friendship, and conflict above compromise. They have lost both the style and substance of the Happy Warrior.

Culture and history often put people in molds that they either cannot or do not break out of. But that was not the case with Ronald Reagan, largely because he lived life imbued by the philosophy of life contained in Henry Wadsworth Longfellow's "Psalm of Life."

Tell me not in mournful numbers,
"Life is but an empty dream!"
For the soul is dead that slumbers,
And things are not what they seem.

Life is real! Life is earnest!
And the grave is not its goal;
"Dust thou art, to dust returnest,"
Was not spoken of the soul.

Not enjoyment, and not sorrow,
Is our destined end or way;
But to act, that each to-morrow
Find us further than to-day.

Art is long, and Time is fleeting,
And our hearts, though stout and brave,
Still, like muffled drums, are beating
Funeral marches to the grave.

In the world's broad field of battle,
In the bivouac of Life,
Be not like dumb, driven cattle!
Be a hero in the strife!

Trust no Future, howe'er pleasant!
Let the dead Past bury its dead!
Act—act in the living Present!
Heart within, and God o'erhead!

Lives of great men all remind us
We can make our lives sublime,
And, departing, leave behind us
Footprints on the sands of time;

Footprints, that perhaps another,
Sailing o'er life's solemn main,
A forlorn and shipwrecked brother,
Seeing, shall take heart again.

Let us, then, be up and doing,
With a heart for any fate;
Still achieving, still pursuing,
Learn to labour and to wait.

NOTES

Epigraph: Thurber quoted in Robert Schmuhl, *Statecraft and Stagecraft: American Political Life in the Age of Personality* (Notre Dame, IN: University of Notre Dame Press, 1990), vii.

1. For an expanded discussion of Reagan's childhood and early life, see Paul Kengor, *God and Ronald Reagan: A Spiritual Life* (New York: HarperCollins, 2005).

2. See Paul Kengor, review of *Reagan, in His Own Hand,* ed. Kiron K. Skinner, Annelise Anderson, and Martin Anderson, *Policy Review,* April–May 2001, http://www.hoover.org/publications/policyreview/3478257.html.

3. Lionel Trilling, *The Liberal Imagination* (New York: Viking, 1950), ix.

4. Stephen Skowronek, *The Politics Presidents Make: Leadership from John Adams to George Bush* (Cambridge, MA: Harvard University Press, 1993), 80.

THE MIXED LEGACIES OF RONALD REAGAN

Hugh Heclo

However friends and foes of Ronald Reagan may parse his life, all must surely agree that he was a remarkable American. They may disagree on the honor due him, but they could hardly deny the significance of his life for good or ill. It is this idea of honoring that I would like to address.

There are different ways of honoring a person. One way is to memorialize him or her. We do that by stamping the person's memory on physical things—a street, a building, an airport, and so on.

Second, we can bestow honor by praising the person. This involves mounting a celebration or similar hortatory project worthy of his or her accomplishments. Here, for example, one might think of Young America's Foundation and Rancho del Cielo.

Finally there is the honor that comes from trying to weigh the consequences of a person having been here in this troubled world—their life deeds. This is the highest form of honoring, because it puts the highest value on the truth of things as best as one can understand them.

Let me suggest that this third form of honoring is especially important, because it requires truth seeking. Of course, even in the best of circumstances, honoring as truth seeking is difficult. A wise man once said that all history is contemporary history. In other words, you and I cannot avoid seeing the past in light of our present. Humanly speaking, that is the only light we have.

If that is the case in the best of circumstances, offering a fair, truthful account of Ronald Reagan's legacy in 2009 is especially difficult. Barely one generation away from his leaving public office, we are only now entering the middle distance necessary for a good historical perspective.

Moreover, Ronald Reagan has obviously become an iconographic figure in our politics. There is a "Reagan legacy industry" that has been at work for some time, and we do now indeed have streets, buildings, and the capital's airport named in his honor. A fair appraisal of his legacy is difficult in today's political climate because partisans on all sides want us to believe that the truth of things must be simple. A mixed verdict on any subject is equated with a betrayal of political purpose.

And yet honoring a person's legacy through seeking the truth of things often requires the kind of complex thinking that today's ruthless partisanship disparages and attacks. The aim of partisanship is to reduce to a minimum the number of things a person needs to think about. My aim is, within reason, to increase that number.

What do we mean by a person's legacy? A legacy is the substance of things passed on. It is an inheritance that is handed to the future and that also, in a sense, handles and shapes that future. In everyday life we experience this idea of a legacy most clearly in our family relationships. For example, we know that parents are always teaching their children, and we also know that what children are learning is often not what was intended. There is an inherent complexity in the idea of a legacy.

- A legacy may amount to something intended as well as unintended.
- It may involve conserving what we have as well as creating something new.
- It may be certain material conditions as well as the perception of those conditions.
- It may develop from what is accomplished as well as what is attempted and failed.

So any person's legacy is a complex thing—or perhaps better stated, it is a complex of things. It requires seriously pondering that intricate braid of continuity and change we are pleased to call history. History has a way of coming around to bite our intentions in the rear end.

Now you can see why I think it is more realistic to speak of the legacies rather than the legacy of Ronald Reagan—and of mixed legacies at that.

Reagan would have recognized these difficulties in speaking and writing about him. He was an essentially humble man, and rather than wanting hagiography, the Gipper would, I think, give his cock of the head and that crinkled, twinkling smile and tell us, "Well, just do your best."

In what follows I will try to draw a sketch of Ronald Reagan's complex legacies. The sketch consists of eight strokes under the headings "America's Welfare State," "Taxation," "National Security," "The Presidency," "Reagan's People," "Party Politics," "Political Leadership," and "The Person."

AMERICA'S WELFARE STATE

In declaring in his first inaugural address that government is the problem, not the solution, Ronald Reagan meant *domestic* government. And he meant not only the size of domestic government but its overbearing ambition to run people's lives. As Reagan put it in his famous 1964 endorsement of Barry Goldwater, Americans' fundamental choice was not between the political Right and Left. Rather it was the choice between up, the ultimate in individual freedom consistent with law and order, and down, to the ant heap of centralized, all-controlling government. In an article in *Reason* magazine, Reagan called the libertarian view of limited government the heart of conservatism.

In practice Ronald Reagan handed down to the future a combination of rhetorical and financial pressures that did restrain the growth of domestic government. But he and his administration did little to enact—or even to prepare the groundwork for—an agenda of limited government. The overall result was to consolidate rather than roll back America's middle-class welfare state. Here we can only briefly review how this occurred.

The Reagan administration did carry forward the government deregulation that had begun under President Jimmy Carter. But it was deregulation that continued to be justified on grounds of economic efficiency and not a conservative-libertarian philosophy of limited government. And when deregulation produced obvious social inefficiencies, as in the savings and loan scandal, reregulation quickly ensued without a nod to any principles of limited government.

President Reagan's calls for private sector charitable initiatives to replace government welfare spending remained short-lived rhetoric in 1981–1982. Likewise his New Federalism proposals to devolve federal welfare entitlements (Aid to Families with Dependent Children [AFDC] and food stamps) to state governments while in return nationalizing Medicare came to nothing.

Challenged on the "fairness issue" after 1981, the president and his spokesmen defended the administration not on grounds of conservative principle but by claiming the government was spending more on food stamps and other welfare programs.

On Social Security, Ronald Reagan had historically favored introducing "voluntary features" into the system but quickly learned to avoid the issue as president. In mid-1981 Reagan suffered his first major presidential setback when a political firestorm arose over his proposal to cut Social Security benefits for those early retirees approaching age sixty-two, a proposal based on short-term budget-balancing needs rather than any social policy principles. In response, President Reagan signed on to establishing a bipartisan commission that would secure the long-term financial future of the Social Security system with no consideration of privatizing or "de-welfarizing" its redistributive features. The outcome of the 1983 reform was to conserve the government's immense entitlement program by future increases in Social Security taxes and the retirement age.

In short, if there ever was anything resembling a frontal assault on the American welfare state by the "Reagan revolution," it had essentially ended by 1982. And even that was not enough to prevent major Republican losses in the midterm elections that year. Rather than teaching Americans anything about a principled commitment to decentralized, limited government, the key to Reagan's 1984 reelection was the scrupulous avoidance of any such substantive issues in favor of mood and personality.

However, the combination of Reagan's fiscal policies and his powerful rhetoric did move the terms of debate toward a generalized hostility to something called "big government." The consequences were typically indirect and paradoxical.

The decades-long rise in federal domestic spending as a percentage of gross domestic product was halted but not reversed and remained roughly stable at about 18 percent after 1982.[1] This was achieved indirectly rather than through frontal assaults on the welfare state. Growth in domestic government's share of the economy was capped in several roundabout ways.

As Reagan and some others intended, growth in domestic government was partly constrained by tax cuts that shrank the revenue stream flowing to Washington. More important, leaving the momentum of huge federal entitlement programs in place and generating ballooning budget deficits served to squeeze domestic programs with politically weak constituencies and made any big new domestic program much more politically costly. Some examples of this legacy are as follows:

- Since they fall into that shrinking share of the federal budget known as nonentitlement discretionary domestic spending, Great Society antipoverty programs have been continually trimmed down.
- Reagan laid the groundwork for the 1989 defeat of the new catastrophic health insurance program for the elderly. To avoid increasing taxes or the deficit, Congress paid for new coverage by charging costs to the program's better-off beneficiaries. This in turn produced a political backlash that forced Congress to repeal the new program.
- By the same logic, Reagan might also be considered the godfather of the subsequent defeat of President Bill Clinton's 1993 health plan. This proposed "managed care" system was easily portrayed as another big government scheme designed to benefit the uninsured minority at the expense of the already insured majority.

The consequence of all this was to solidify America's middle-class welfare state with minimal public education in, or commitment to, principles of limited government. Misreading this fact, Newt Gingrich and his fellow "anti–welfare state" revolutionaries who took over Congress in 1994 were easy political prey. A 1995 shutdown of "big government" and proposed budget cuts allowed President Clinton to portray congressional Republicans as enemies of the government's social safety net, particularly the Medicare system, on which parents of the middle class depended. This in turn gave major aid to Clinton's reelection in 1996.[2]

Thus it is part of Reagan's legacy that neither Americans at large nor even Republican politicians were ultimately weaned from dependence on big government. Under a Republican Congress, from 1994 to 2006, the number of earmarks for special federal spending projects tripled. Under a Republican president and Congress, the first years of the twenty-first century saw the largest expansion of federal education policy in history as well as the creation of a huge new Washington entitlement program for prescription drugs. Surveys found that by 2005, roughly one-third of the Republican coalition deserved the odd label "pro-government conservatives," that is, Republican voters favoring federal government activism on any number of domestic issues.[3]

There is a final irony flowing from Reagan's nonrevolution in social policy. Frustrated by the Reagan administration's accommodations, especially on Social Security, conservatives outside Congress sought a new strategy to produce "real reform"—that is, privatization—in Social Security. They crafted an approach that would have the political allure of holding existing beneficiaries harmless while promising young future retirees a better return through personal investment accounts. This was essentially the proposal on which President George W. Bush squandered what he called his "political capital" after winning reelection in 2004.

The legacy problem for any potential Reagan revolution against the welfare state is that in our democracy, over the long run, the government tends to do what the people want. Facing economic and social insecurities, people want the things government can do for them, even if in some abstract philosophical sense they could do those things for themselves. In that sense, people want the anthill.

TAXATION

In Reagan's own view, changes in federal tax policy constituted a major part of his legacy. As he put it in his memoir, "With the tax cuts of 1981 and the Tax Reform Act of 1986, I'd accomplished a lot of what I'd come to Washington to do."[4] There is a widespread perception, encouraged by subsequent conservative commentators and Republican politicians, that by pursuing a vigorous policy of cutting taxes, Reagan unleashed the productive energies that, from 1983 to 1989, produced the longest period of continuous economic growth in American history. However, the actual Reagan tax legacy has been a good deal more complicated.

Some things Ronald Reagan wanted have endured. The deep, across-the-board reduction of federal income tax rates of 1981 has remained largely intact. So too has the cut in the top marginal tax rate (70 percent when he took office, 28 percent when he left, and 35 percent now). Likewise, the indexing of tax rate brackets has prevented inflation from automatically pushing taxpayers at all levels into higher brackets. The Tax

Reform Act of 1986, which Reagan championed, did produce a major broadening of the base in the federal income tax by eliminating a mass of tax deductions, exemptions, and credits for special interests, especially business tax shelters. It also removed 6 million low-income workers from income tax liability. Since then more loopholes have crept back into the tax code, but much of the general broadening of the income tax base has endured.

Nonetheless, Reagan's efforts did not change other central features of federal taxation. As a percentage of national income, the federal government's role in extracting tax resources from the economy remained essentially unchanged during the 1980s (19.4 percent in 1980 and 19.3 percent in 1989). This is because, having in 1981 achieved the largest tax cut in American history, President Reagan in 1982 and 1984 signed some of the largest tax increases in American history to try to cope with the ballooning budget deficit.

Likewise, despite partisan claims to the contrary, the progressivity of the federal tax system changed little as a result of Reagan's tax policies. Since they pay the largest dollar amounts in taxes, taxpayers at the highest income levels naturally have gained the most from cuts in the top marginal income tax rates. But across the whole range of the income distribution, the effective federal tax rate from the lowest to the highest fifth of families scarcely budged from 1980 to 1991.[5]

Taking a broader view, it seems fair to say that the stimulus for continued economic growth after 1983 came less from tax reductions and more from the huge federal budget deficits produced by Reagan's defense buildup and the maintenance of the large domestic entitlement programs. Added together over the Reagan years, these deficits tripled the national debt and helped keep the economy growing.

Reagan's unrelenting rhetoric on the harmful effects of federal taxes had important consequences for political perceptions. It helped make new or increased taxes to pay for programs a no-go area for all other politicians down to the present day. In the long run, Reagan's presidency probably enhanced Americans' deficit tolerance as well as their tax aversion. They were taught to indulge their already well-developed habit of short-term thinking. Profits from the U.S. trade deficit could be used by foreigners to purchase the federal debt financing our budget deficits. Americans could consume and Washington could spend without anyone having to pay their way through higher taxes. We have yet to face up to that legacy. We have a $13 trillion economy. Eight years ago the nation's total liabilities and unfunded commitments were $20 trillion. In 2008, they were $53 trillion.

Although Ronald Reagan always publicly advocated the virtues of a balanced budget, when it came time to choose, holding the line on deficits always lost out to his other priorities. Vice President Dick Cheney was making a political, not an economic, point when he allegedly argued during George W. Bush's administration, "Reagan proved deficits don't matter."[6] Reagan showed that the public did not punish or reward politicians because they increased or decreased the deficit. The red ink didn't seem to matter.

However, there was, and remains, a political short-sightedness in Cheney's lesson drawing. Eventually the growing deficit led to the 1990 budget crisis and the breaking of the "Read my lips—no new taxes" promise that wrecked George H. W. Bush's presidency among Reagan Republicans. The mounting deficit also helped launch the third-party candidacy of Ross Perot. Together, these political reactions in turn probably sheared off enough Republican votes in 1992 to put Bill Clinton in the White House. Such are the ironies in assessing a political legacy.

The long view yields a final irony. President Reagan's success in cutting income tax rates and broadening the tax base helped defuse hostility to a federal income tax system that had increasingly been seen as burdensome and unfair. Lower individual rates made the system appear less onerous, and the 1986 reform removing special preferences made it seem fairer. The ultimate consequence was to shore up the political acceptability of our current federal income tax system. By doing so, Reagan helped make less likely any more fundamental tax reforms, such as a flat tax or consumption tax. To the frustration of many conservatives, that stabilization of the status quo continues today.

NATIONAL SECURITY

For many years into the future, scholars will be debating Ronald Reagan's legacy in ending the cold war. That is not an issue we can hope to settle here.

What we can do is identify some long-term implications of Reagan's approach to national security policy. It was a distinctive and remarkably consistent approach throughout his political career. In important respects it flew in the face of the prevailing opinion. But eventually Reagan bent much of that opinion in his direction.

Throughout his political career, Reagan remained almost exclusively focused on the threat to America's security posed by the Soviet Union and its aggressive Communist ideology. In three essential ways, he came to Washington rejecting the cold war as he found it—and as most experts and opinion leaders thought it must be.

First, Reagan rejected the notion that America's ultimate response to the Communist threat should be containment or détente. The goal was defeat of this enemy and victory for the cause of freedom, which is humanity's as well as America's cause. His critics viewed this commitment to victory as lacking subtlety. Reagan, on the other hand, viewed Communism as an inherently aggressive form of insanity that violated human nature and must one day disappear. The goal was not to manage and coexist with the global Soviet threat. America's goal should be to defeat that threat peacefully.

Second, Reagan was equally clear that to preserve peace and the nation's security, the United States must have unquestioned military strength. He rejected the consensus that sought an equilibrium of power backed by arms control treaties with the Soviets. Communists' unchanging goal of world domination and disdain for treaty promises meant that peace could be had in only one of two ways: either by surrendering or by making America stronger than its adversary. Reagan opted for peace through superior strength, both militarily and economically.

Finally, Reagan rejected the prevailing doctrine of deterrence through mutually assured destruction. As he came to see it, the promise of offensive retaliation to deter a Soviet attack was not a genuine defense. After years of building their military advantage, Russian leaders thought a nuclear war was both possible and winnable. A genuine defense against nuclear attack would protect the American people rather than simply avenge them. Hence Reagan's defense buildup broke with conventional thinking to include the Strategic Defense Initiative, which would render Soviet nuclear weaponry a useless expenditure.

Critics saw Reagan's expansive defense spending as provocative warmongering that would lead to an exploding arms race. Reagan saw superior military strength, including the new missile defense system, as a way of forcing Soviet leaders to the bargaining table to make real concessions. Contrary to what some people think, Reagan did not change course when Gorbachev appeared on the scene. His goal had always been to reduce nuclear weapons with verifiable agreements, to the point where neither side represented a threat to the other.

It is a central part of Reagan's legacy that these three features were the general terms on which the cold war ended after he left office. Besides this monumental fact, there were other consequences of Reagan's approach to national security that deserve notice.

Reagan saw that rebuilding American military dominance could only be the reflection of a deeper rebuilding of the American spirit, which had become demoralized in the 1960s and 1970s. There first had to be the national will to prevail. And that depended on Americans' conviction that they deserved to prevail. Recalling Americans to that moral rearmament was Reagan's primary teaching achievement in advancing the nation's security. It is what he meant by "bringing America back."

The moral clarity Reagan espoused in fighting Communism was an influential precedent for President George W. Bush and neoconservatives in his administration's war on terrorism. Sharp divisions between friend and foe, good and evil, became the watchword. Likewise, Reagan's vision of a global mission in defeating Communism strained almost to the breaking point the caution, modesty, and anti-utopianism that Russell Kirk had commended as the conservative approach to America's duties in the world.[7] As Reagan's would-be heir, President George W. Bush pushed past those bounds of conservative restraint, presenting American-backed democracy as a sure antidote to terrorism.

There were other national security legacies. The cold war was the lens through which Reagan saw all defense and foreign policy issues, and this produced certain blind spots. Two have had major long-term implications.

First, the Reagan doctrine sought to roll back whatever might be seen as Communist influence throughout the third world. This led to American support for brutal regimes and proxy wars that had nothing to do with moral clarity and everything to do with whatever seemed expedient as an anti-Soviet maneuver. The negative consequences were profound.

To support the contras in Nicaragua, Reagan embraced the murderous government of Rios Montt in Guatemala. To counter Communist influence in Africa, the Reagan White House welcomed Angola's Jonas Savimbi and his no less murderous UNITA forces. Partly for the same reason, President Reagan rejected sanctions against South Africa's apartheid regime and praised the anti-Communist stance of its segregated tribal "republics." Because it had been ousted by the pro-Soviet Vietnamese government, Cambodia's Khmer Rouge found the Reagan administration championing its recognition as a government in exile at the United Nations. With Donald Rumsfeld as his Middle East envoy, Reagan removed Saddam Hussein's Iraq from the list of state sponsors of terrorism and gave the dictator major weapons supplies, not only to protract the brutal war with Iran but also to thwart the pro-Soviet Syrian regime of Hafez al-Assad. And in Afghanistan, the trickle of weapons sent to the mujahideen under President Carter became a massive weapons flow to radical Islamic forces fighting to expel the Soviets.

This brings us to the second major consequence of conflating all threats to American security as a single menace of Communist aggression. Reagan was largely blind to the threat of militant Islam. He simply melded Islamic radicalism into Communist imperialism. Thus in 1985 Reagan denounced five countries—Cuba, Nicaragua, North Korea, Iran, and Libya—as a united front of terrorist states. In 1986 he pressed Congress for renewed support for the anti-Sandinista "freedom fighters" by invoking the vision of Communist Nicaragua becoming a sanctuary for "Muammar Qaddafi, Arafat and the Ayatollah," who would lap America's southern borders in "a sea of red."[8]

Reagan was equally blind to how his administration's actions, supposedly against "leftists," were inadvertently fueling a threat from radical Islamic groups. Thus as Menachem Begin and Ariel Sharon sought to finally eliminate the Palestine Liberation Organization, Reagan was surprised and reluctantly drawn into backing the Israeli invasion of Lebanon in June 1982. Early in September Reagan defended Sharon's bombing and shelling of Muslim neighborhoods as a response to "leftist militias," an Israeli allegation that the State Department was quickly forced to deny. To Reagan's disgust, Israeli forces then facilitated the massacre of Muslim families in West Beirut. In response, the U.S. Marines returned to Beirut as a so-called multinational peacekeeping force to keep a peace that did not exist. From there it was all downhill. With marine peacekeepers prohibited from using their weapons in what was now a civil war, the U.S. Navy tried to provide offshore support to the marines' position at the Beirut airport by shelling Muslim militias in the Shiite slums and surrounding mountains.

This reality of hostile military engagements in Lebanon was denied by Reagan, lest the War Powers Act of 1973 should be invoked and signal weakness to the Soviet Union and its Syrian ally. A tight chain of events, unexplained to the American public, now snapped into place. Israel's invasion and occupation of Lebanon, the massacre of Muslims in West Beirut, and the U.S. Navy's bombardment of Muslim neighborhoods could now be linked in many Muslims' minds to justify the retaliatory suicide bombings of the U.S. embassy and U.S. Marines barracks in Beirut in April and October 1983. The same linkage, of which Americans were left oblivious, produced the hijacking of TWA flight 847 in June 1985, the subsequent holding of seven hostages from that flight, and Reagan's ill-fated attempt to free these and other Americans in Beirut through an arms-for-hostages deal, using Iran as the middleman. More on this in a moment.

Certainly it was not Reagan's intention to present the United States as an imperialist, anti-Islamic power. But, just as certainly, this was a perception that grew and spread throughout the Muslim world in the 1980s. In the end, the Reagan administration did much to aid the growing cause of radical jihadists in the Middle East.

All this notwithstanding, the benefits of hindsight should not obscure a central point. The threat posed by Soviet Communism and nuclear war was the primary danger to Americans' security in Reagan's day. He successfully answered that historic challenge.

THE PRESIDENCY

Ronald Reagan's legacy for the institution of the presidency presents its own mixed image.

On the one hand, Reagan revived an executive office that was in a weak, dispirited condition. In the twenty years before 1980, Americans had lived through five traumatic, and what many considered to be failed, presidencies. There was also a growing opinion that the presidency might be just too much for one man to handle.

After two terms, Reagan left behind a presidency that was robust and widely admired. One sign is that President Clinton, trying to revive his own presidency after 1994, allegedly studied videotapes of Ronald Reagan in an attempt to imitate his bearing, maturity, and aura of command. Vice President Al Gore did the same in preparing to debate George W. Bush in 2000.

Another sign is the effectiveness with which Reagan put his imprint on executive branch operations. This occurred through more centralized White House scrutiny of departmental personnel decisions and budgets, judicial appointments, federal regulations, and "signing statements" that challenged particular features of laws the president was signing.

Beyond that, if political scientists are to be believed, successful presidents lead through exercising their power to persuade. They combine an active, transformative agenda and a positive, uplifting attitude. President Reagan fulfilled that bill of particulars. He brought dignity, confidence, and moral conviction to the office. He brought a vision that helped restore America's confidence in itself.

All of this belongs on the positive side of the ledger.

On the other hand, Reagan also passed on a presidency that was more dangerous for our constitutional order, although that obviously was never his intention. It was the accidental disclosure of the Iran-contra affair that brought this danger to light. The surrounding events not only reaffirmed the public perception of big lies in high places but also showed a tolerance for presidential actions that directly contradicted congressional authorizations and legal statutes.

Media attention to the diversion of funds from Iran to the Nicaraguan contras was actually a diversion from the central issue.[9] This issue was the illegal activity involved both in supplying the contras and in selling arms to Iran in the first place. Beginning in the summer of 1984, Reagan and key aides evaded the legal requirements for covert operations laid down by congressional statute as well as by the president's own executive order and national security directive. This evasion of the law was then concealed by false or misleading statements given to the public and Congress by the president and his spokesmen.

Similar evasion and concealment then accelerated through covert arms sales to Iran authorized by the president. Such sales were clearly illegal under the Arms Control Export Act of 1976 and the 1979 U.S. arms embargo against Iran, which designated that nation a supporter of international terrorism. Further requirements for reporting to Congress under the National Security Act of 1947 were then deliberately violated by senior administration officials.

There was nothing conservative about such disregard for the institutional values of a constitutional government under law. Nonetheless, the Iran-contra affair now gave impetus in some Republican circles to expansive claims of inherent executive power, and this too became part of the Reagan presidential legacy. Congressman Dick Cheney and his young aide David Addington led a spirited defense of Reagan's actions. In this view, the primary role in the conduct of foreign policy rested with a presidency enjoying minimal congressional interference. On occasion the president could even use his prerogative power to "exceed the law."[10]

On this reading, the Iran-contra scandal simply represented a partisan effort by congressional Democrats to seize powers that legitimately belonged to the presidency. A new mission was set in motion among a cadre of neoconservatives: to reverse an alleged infringement of presidential power that had occurred following the Vietnam War and the Watergate scandal. Some fifteen years later, Cheney, now as vice president, with Addington heading his legal team, was in a position to lead the Bush administration's effort to claim inherent executive powers—some of which included imprisonment, surveillance, interrogation, and possibly torture.[11]

In considering whether Ronald Reagan was a "great president," we should use those words very carefully. Taken alone, "greatness" simply means to be marked by outstanding merit. However, to be a great president is an inherently constitutional idea. It is to excel in the context of a constitutional office, in this case the office holding the executive power. "Office" in its original, most meaningful sense has to do with obligations to act by virtue of being positioned in a certain place. The concept of "office" is about occupying not a physical place but a moral space in the political order.

During his last months in the White House, Reagan observed, "You don't become president of the United States. You are given temporary custody of an institution called the presidency, which belongs to our people."[12] But this is not quite right. The institution does not belong to the people, not directly. It belongs to the Constitution, which is the creation of the people.

There are only two promises in the presidential oath: to execute the duties of the office and to safeguard the Constitution. For all his positive contributions to the presidency, Reagan did not demonstrate outstanding merit in the context of the executive office known to the Constitution. Legacies teach things, and Reagan did not teach us well about the executive power in our constitutional order. His zeal for rolling back Communist influence in Central America and his personal concern for the hostage situation led him and his aides into the extraconstitutional and illegal activities of the Iran-contra affair.

In the end, most Americans seemed willing to forgive the Gipper as merely uninformed or forgetful. But a constitutionally perilous legacy had been created. In asserting executive power, Reagan and his officials violated congressional laws and the spirit of the Constitution. And equally clearly, they largely got away with it as a precedent for future years. The American presidency was left stronger, more manageable, and more dangerous.

REAGAN'S PEOPLE

Before and during his eight years in the White House, Ronald Reagan carried with him into the public arena major portions of America's next generation of leaders, conservative and otherwise. This easily overlooked matter of personnel is also a part of his legacy.

The courts are an example. By the end of his two terms, Ronald Reagan had appointed almost half of all federal judges (as well as three Supreme Court justices). His judicial selection process centered in the White House also had done much to ensure that these judges were people, mostly fairly young, with a reputation for legal conservatism. These almost four hundred judges in the federal district and appeals courts will be with us for some years to come.

Beyond the obvious example of the courts, it is easy to overlook the fine-grained nature of Reagan's personnel legacy. It consists of quietly shaping the career lines of hundreds of individuals over the years. In this group are Robert Gates, John Negroponte, Colin Powell, Dennis Ross, Paul Wolfowitz, and Jeane Kirkpatrick, to name only a few prominent figures in the realm of foreign affairs. Other career lines in Congress, state governments, think tanks, foundations, and the like are also part of this immense, untold story.

Reagan's farthest-reaching legacy in the realm of personnel deserves a few more specific comments.

By choosing him as his running mate (Gerald Ford disdained the offer), Reagan breathed new life into the all but expired political career of George H. W. Bush. With only two terms in the House and two defeats in running for Senate, Bush's own elective record was lackluster, and his conservative credentials had long been suspect among the movement's activists, including Ronald Reagan.

After Goldwater's 1964 loss, the political newcomer Reagan publicly challenged George Bush's view that conservatives should now make their home in a big-tent GOP. Reagan, like Russell Kirk, saw the 1964 election as a sign that the GOP could be a thoroughly conservative party representing the majority of forgotten Americans.[13] In the years after 1964, Bush advanced up the political ladder by retailing his personal contacts. Reagan advanced by wholesaling his personal beliefs. When the young George W. Bush ran for Congress in 1978, Ronald Reagan endorsed his opponent in the Republican primary as the truer conservative. And in the 1980 presidential primaries, Reagan defeated Bush Sr.'s brand of a more moderate, mainstream Republicanism. As Bush told one of his speechwriters during those primaries, "Jamie, I'm a Republican—isn't that enough. . . . I like Barry Goldwater, but stuff like his *Conscience of a Conservative* isn't my thing."[14]

As he had in tapping liberal Pennsylvania senator Richard Schweiker as his running mate in 1976, Reagan behaved as a prudent politician in choosing Bush in 1980. And in choosing Bush's campaign manager, James Baker, as White House chief of staff, Reagan showed he recognized and was not threatened by talented people who were not movement conservatives. The fact remains, however, that Ronald Reagan did not work to secure a succession of conservative leadership for the Republican Party. As Reagan's running mate, Bush Sr. obtained the inside track for the Republican presidential nomination after Reagan left office.

Likewise, young George W. gained his first national political experience in helping with his father's revived political prospects. With Bush's campaign to succeed Reagan, which the family began planning in early 1985, the young George Bush became a senior, full-time adviser working with the brilliant star of Republican political consultants, Lee Atwater. And so it was that a few months after President Bush left the White House in 1993, a new generation of Team Bush had assembled in Texas to launch George W.'s run for the governorship, which in turn became a stepping-stone to the White House.

Thus Ronald Reagan, however inadvertently, set in motion forces that would eventually produce twelve years of Bush presidencies and a gradual unraveling of the conservative coalition.

Party Politics

As others have ably described, Ronald Reagan used the political materials lying around him to build a conservative coalition that was unprecedented in modern American politics. What was this creative work's legacy for our party system?

Clearly the electoral strength of Reagan's coalition has not been as deep or durable as FDR's Democratic coalition. During the Reagan and Bush presidencies, Republicans never managed to gain full control of Congress, and they lost the two presidential elections of the 1990s. Apparent turning points in 1980 (when Reagan received only 51 percent of the popular vote) and 1994 (in congressional elections) had more to do with public disgust directed toward Democratic incumbents in the White House and Congress than with any widespread endorsement of a conservative agenda (although of course winners always claimed such a positive mandate). In 1982, twenty-six House Republican seats were lost, including those of fourteen freshmen who had just arrived on Reagan's coattails. The reelection of three anti-Reagan Republican mavericks (David Durenberger, John Chafee, and Lowell Weicker) helped keep the Senate in Republican hands. Following his 1984 landslide reelection, President Reagan campaigned for Republicans in ten Senate races in 1986, including five in the South. Democrats won all ten Senate seats.

In short, the "realigning" election that pundits kept looking for never happened.

Nevertheless, Ronald Reagan did bequeath enduring changes to our party system. In terms of Americans' identification with a political party, the Republicans now overcame their half-century status as a minority party. By the end of the 1980s, Republican Party identifiers were roughly equal to Democratic Party identifiers, and so they have remained. Young white Americans who came of age during the Reagan years have proven a distinctively Republican and conservative political generation. Thus Reagan laid the groundwork for the closely divided, 50/50 electoral nation that we experience today.

The more equal division of support between the two parties also brought with it a sharper ideological division. As Reagan had doggedly sought since 1964, the Republicans became a more thoroughly conservative party. And in making the Republican Party a conservative party, Reagan also changed the way Americans saw conservatism. In 1964 it had seemed antiquated, negative, and dangerously radical. By 1988 conservatism was more likely to be seen as Reaganesque—forward looking, optimistic, and in the mainstream of American values.

At least as significant was the fact that Reagan's conservative coalition offered leaders of evangelical Christians their first sustained entrée onto the national political scene since the days of William Jennings Bryan. Grassroots organization and division on cultural issues made the Republicans a more overtly religious party. Activists in both parties found it profitable to emphasize this division and demonize their opponents. In effect, both the Republican and Democratic parties became more effective sorting mechanisms for organizing Bible-believing Americans and more strictly secular Americans into two different camps.

While liberal activists continued to fight against it, Reagan also shifted the center of the Democratic Party toward the pragmatic, if not philosophical, right. Reagan's legacy, again an indirect one, was to supply a competitive advantage to ambitious Democratic politicians with more supple personal views. Hence Bill Clinton could emerge as a "New Democrat" because the old Democrats could not come up with a plausible alternative to Ronald Reagan.

POLITICAL LEADERSHIP

Elsewhere I have written about Reagan's importance for what some call America's public philosophy, and I will not repeat that here. Instead let me turn to another part of his legacy that is too often overlooked—his reaffirmation and elevation of the politician's role in a democracy.

Reagan's harshest critics declared him to be a simple-minded ideologue. Some who worked with him, such as David Stockman, found Reagan to be "a consensus politician, not an ideologue."[15] For his own part, Reagan often liked to portray himself as an ordinary citizen in office.

The truth of the matter is something larger than these partial views. Reagan's political leadership exemplified the high calling of the politician in a democracy.

Americans want political leaders who are both principled and effective. There is, of course, an underlying tension between these two characteristics. The principled leader is idealistic, straightforward, and firm. The effective leader in our messy democratic system is pragmatic, flexible, and at times duplicitous. At their best, democratic political leaders manage that tension without fostering public cynicism. This is what Reagan accomplished, and in doing so, he set a long-term example for other would-be leaders.

Ronald Reagan did not enter politics at age fifty-five because his ego needed votes or public office. He did it because he believed deeply in certain very important things. And throughout his political career, people seemed to perceive and like this about him. I think this public understanding goes a long way to explain his remarkable appeal even in the most unfavorable circumstances. As his presidency was ending, only Ronald Reagan could have gotten away with these lines: "A few months ago I told the American people I did not trade arms for hostages. My heart and my best intentions still tell me that's true, but the facts and the evidence tell me it is not."[16]

Reagan was what George Will has called a "conviction politician." He effectively communicated and firmly adhered to core principles. But he was also willing eventually to compromise to make partial advances toward his goals. This principled pragmatism irritates those wanting ideological purity. But it is of priceless value for a healthy democracy. Reagan probably did weaken the conservative movement by investing it with governing responsibility and the adulterated purity that governing entails. But the gain for our democratic way of life in having such political leadership far outweighs that cost.

The gain is that Ronald Reagan exemplified the high calling of a democratic politician to find the working terms on which government by consent can go forward. This is the essential thing for a diverse people who hope to be self-governing—principled leadership that knows how to mediate, adjust, and continue discovering the basis on which people will live together.

Reagan also showed how a politician with honest convictions does not need to slur his political rivals' character, competence, or good intentions. Instead, Reagan invariably sought to teach listeners how his rivals misunderstood the real problems and what a truer understanding required. Reagan set an example of democratic leadership that is available for other would-be politicians to follow, if they only will.

THE PERSON

As we come to the end of this sketch, the last stroke is possibly the most important. This is because Reagan's legacy is something more than a sum of the parts I have outlined. It is a legacy that has to do with the whole person. Reagan's is an influence that goes very deep because it can evade our consciousness.

In the long term, history does not give points for style. It is not the style but the substance of the man we are talking about here. Reagan's basis for being the so-called Great Communicator was not style. What Reagan communicated to people was that he believed what he said. And what he believed was hopeful. Some have said that Ronald Reagan made America feel good about itself. This is true, but it would be wrong to characterize this as a fluffy, feel-good message.

The hopefulness Reagan believed in and communicated was deeply rooted in America's revolutionary and religious traditions. Reagan was a visionary traditionalist and thus a futurist as well. The "old" truths were always new because they were forever lifting free people to new possibilities. As he said in his presidential farewell address, what people called the Reagan revolution was really "the great rediscovery, a rediscovery of our values and our common sense."[17]

Part of the appealing romance of Ronald Reagan's life is its paradoxical nature. He recalled citizens to a vision of traditional values in small-town America, to unapologetic patriotism and the simple virtues of ordinary people. And yet Reagan built his career in the modern world of mass entertainment. He emerged from the media-driven, corporate structures of Hollywood and TV. Precisely these forces were challenging the social, economic, and cultural ligaments of traditional, small-town American life, but Reagan conceptualized a world different from the way it was. As Senator Edward Kennedy said, Reagan "stood for a set of ideas. . . . He meant them—and he wrote most of them not only into public law but into the national consciousness."[18]

When Reagan told Americans the good things they wanted to believe about themselves and their nation, this was no subterfuge or political strategy. He did it because he believed that he was—at the deepest level—telling them the truth about themselves. But he was also communicating the truth about himself. Within the man were basic decency, kindness, hopefulness, and principled toughness. These were what he saw in America itself. In this regard his legacy is what he hoped for. "Whatever else history may say about me when I'm gone," he said, "I hope it will record that I appealed to your best hopes, not your worst fears."[19]

We puny commentators, offering our historical verdicts so far from the scene of battle, will soon be forgotten. Ronald Reagan will not.

This is because there was an American romance about Reagan's life, and an American poetry in his vision. He was a lover who saw heroic, good, beautiful things about this nation. He saw and loved the light it shed for freedom-loving people, pilgrims, as he put it, "from all the lost places who are hurtling through the darkness, toward home."[20] Of all the things I have discussed, perhaps the greatest thing Reagan bequeathed was the legacy of his person, an American image that will continue to inspire untold numbers of people. It is as if they will hear that velvety voice saying, in the words of T. E. Lawrence,

I loved you, so I drew these tides of men into my hands
and wrote my will across the sky in stars.[21]

NOTES

1. C. Eugene Steuerle, Edward N. Gramlich, Hugh Heclo, and Demetra S. Nightingale, *The Government We Deserve: Responsive Democracy and Changing Expectations* (Washington, DC: Urban Institute Press, 1998), 66.

2. The strongest counterargument to my general theme here is the issue of welfare reform. One can legitimately claim that Reagan's criticism of the federal AFDC welfare system when he was a governor and a presidential candidate did lead the way for the 1996 replacement of this entitlement program with state-based temporary assistance programs with strong work requirements. Here too, however, the legacy is more complex. As president, Reagan never sought fundamental reform of the AFDC system and, in 1988, signed on to an essentially Democratic bill (Senator Moynihan's Family Support Act). This law increased the federal government's spending and state governments' obligations to provide welfare clients with training, health care, and transportation services, with only the barest of work requirements. The actual stimulus for the fundamental 1996 welfare reform came from granting waivers of federal AFDC rules to particular states, allowing them to experiment with work requirements, benefit cutoffs, and other requirements emphasizing personal responsibility. This waiver process was something of an afterthought in the Reagan administration. The authority for waivers to encourage work was broadened through a small provision in the massive Omnibus Budget Reconciliation Act of 1981. An obscure White House board created by Reagan in 1987 overruled the Department of Health and Human Services to grant New Jersey and Wisconsin extensive waivers for work requirements and benefit cutoffs. This precedent

was extended to over two dozen states in the following years and established the political and analytic basis for eliminating the AFDC entitlement in 1996.

3. Pew Research Center for the People and the Press, *The 2005 Political Typology,* http://people-press.org/reports/pdf/242.pdf.

4. Ronald Reagan, *An American Life* (New York: Simon and Schuster, 1990), 335.

5. It is estimated that those in the lowest fifth of the income distribution had an effective federal tax rate of 8.4 percent in 1980 and 8.5 percent in 1991; those in the top fifth had a rate of 26.8 percent in 1980 and 27.3 percent in 1991. Congressional Budget Office data cited in W. Elliot Brownlee and C. Eugene Steuerle, "Taxation," in *The Reagan Presidency: Pragmatic Conservatism and Its Legacies,* ed. W. Elliot Brownlee and Hugh Davis Graham (Lawrence: University Press of Kansas, 2003), 181n64. I have drawn on this excellent volume as the source for a number of issues discussed in this chapter.

6. Cheney quoted in Ron Suskind, *The Price of Loyalty: George W. Bush, the White House, and the Education of Paul O'Neill* (New York: Simon and Schuster, 2004).

7. Russell Kirk, *The Conservative Mind* (N.p.: BN, 2008), 424.

8. Reagan quoted in Richard Reeves, *President Reagan: The Triumph of Imagination* (New York: Simon and Schuster, 2005), 313.

9. That the diversion of funds was a deliberate White House strategy to divert attention from the more serious misdeeds is suggested in Oliver L. North with William Novak, *Under Fire: An American Story* (New York: HarperCollins, 1992), 7–8.

10. Representative Dick Cheney and four members of the House and two senators, minority report, *Report of the Congressional Committees Investigating the Iran-Contra Affair,* 110th Cong., 1st sess., November 1987, 665. The subsequent implications are analyzed in James P. Pfiffner, *Power Play: The Bush Presidency and the Constitution* (Washington, DC: Brookings Institution Press, 2008).

11. See Charlie Savage, *Takeover: The Return of the Imperial Presidency and the Subversion of American Democracy* (New York: Little, Brown, 2007).

12. Ronald Reagan, address to the Republican National Convention (New Orleans, LA, August 15, 1988), Public Papers of President Ronald W. Reagan, Ronald Reagan Presidential Library, http://www.reagan.utexas.edu/archives/speeches/publicpapers.html. (hereafter cited as Reagan Papers).

13. *National Review,* December 1, 1964, 1053–56.

14. Bush quoted in James C. Humes, *Confessions of a White House Ghostwriter* (Washington, DC: Regnery, 1997), 177.

15. David A. Stockman, *The Triumph of Politics: How the Reagan Revolution Failed* (New York: Harper and Row, 1986), 9.

16. Ronald Reagan, address to the nation on the Iran arms and contra aid controversy (Washington, DC, March 4, 1987), Reagan Papers.

17. Ronald Reagan, farewell address to the nation (Washington, DC, January 11, 1989), Reagan Papers.

18. Kennedy quoted in Charles Krauthammer, "He Could See for Miles," *Time*, June 7, 2004, http://www.time.com/time/columnist/krauthammer/article/0,9565,646538,00.html.

19. Ronald Reagan, address to the Republican National Convention (Houston, TX, August 17, 1992), Reagan Papers.

20. Reagan, farewell address.

21. T. E. Lawrence, *Seven Pillars of Wisdom: A Triumph* (New York: Anchor, 1991), n.p.

THE SOCIAL CONSTRUCTION OF RONALD REAGAN

James W. Ceaser

Not so long ago, Ronald Reagan was laid to rest on a hillside in Simi Valley, overlooking the Pacific Ocean. The burial, together with the extensive ceremonial observances preceding it in Washington, held the nation's attention for a full four days. Considering both Ronald Reagan's age and his condition at the time of his death, these events were not marked by a sense of tragedy. Instead, they became a national commemoration, even a celebration, the largest such event since V-J day. During this time, old foes of Ronald Reagan for the most part either maintained a decent silence or, in a few instances, expressed a qualified admiration for the deceased ex-president.

Not all of this respect or praise, it now seems, was sincere. Just when many began to think that the long and bitter partisan contest over Ronald Reagan's legacy had finally been settled—and settled generally in his favor—the 2008 presidential campaign made clear that Ronald Reagan remains a polarizing figure in American politics. The presidential candidate Barack Obama's descriptive remark that "Ronald Reagan changed the trajectory of America in a way that Richard Nixon . . . and Bill Clinton did not," provoked a maelstrom of criticism from his Democratic competitors, who pronounced it a sin not to speak ill of Ronald Reagan. Never one to miss an occasion to foment class division, John Edwards declared, "He [Reagan] did extraordinary damage to the middle class and working class . . . and caused the middle class and working people to struggle every single day. . . . I can promise you this: this president will never use Ronald Reagan as an example for change." Here was one promise that John Edwards would keep.

The ease with which this anti-Reagan sentiment could be ignited as a political issue in a Democratic presidential nomination race, twenty years after Reagan left office, was striking. Only slightly less so was the continuing adulation that Republicans expressed for Ronald Reagan. Challenged by many in his party about his conservative credentials, John McCain sought to mollify these concerns by reminding Republicans that he had entered politics as "a foot soldier in the Reagan army." When all is said and done, therefore, the underlying ideological structure of American politics that Ronald Reagan helped to shape still appears to be basically intact. Although cracks in the edifice are evident as voters slip from the old moorings (especially younger voters for whom Reagan is a distant figure from the past), no viable, alternative ideological way of thinking has yet been offered to take its place. America is still living in the Reagan era. And the contest over Ronald Reagan's legacy continues.

POSTMODERNISM AND LEGACY MANAGEMENT

The title "The Social Construction of Ronald Reagan" has a decidedly postmodern ring to it. "Social construction" is a concept that is very much in vogue, especially among fashionable literary critics and degree holders in sociology. It is often used to suggest that there is no reality, that nothing that is is, except as we humans make it so. Everything, as the saying now goes, is "constructed," with the aim usually of promoting the constructors' self-serving ends (a fact they attempt to conceal). The theory of social construction has its own view of the world and its own cosmology: in the beginning man created spin.

There is something pleasantly paradoxical in the idea of spin or construction. Spin obviously works best, from the spinner's point of view, when it is perceived not as spin but as an honest effort at describing reality. Nothing poses a greater challenge to the spinner than to be placed publicly in a "spin room," a location that already heavily discounts the sincerity of his remarks. The cleverest spinner would be one who could have people believe that he was operating from a no-spin zone. Yet the most radical theories of social construction deny that such a position is possible. With all apologies to Bill O'Reilly, there is no such thing.

Am I so sophisticated as to subscribe fully to this skeptical view of the world? I hope that I do not disappoint too many if I enter a qualification, one prompted by my embarrassment in encountering colleagues who have written notable biographies of someone named Ronald Wilson Reagan. These authors have staked their credibility on the claim that this personage was not "constructed" but was a real living and breathing individual. Not only do I join with them in acknowledging this proposition as simple fact, but I would also accede to the bolder contention that Ronald Reagan served as the fortieth president of the United States.

Yet I also think these fine scholars would be among the first to agree that, besides their own efforts as genuine biographers to discover the truth about Ronald Reagan, a parallel activity has been going on to influence the reputation of Ronald Reagan for the purpose of exercising a political effect. And they would also, I am sure, agree with me that many of those engaged in this activity are, if not wholly oblivious of the truth, willing to torture or shade it if that will help to promote their goal. Some indeed may even be doing this unconsciously, so blinded have they become by their partisan dispositions. It is this activity of creating and influencing reputations for political purposes, or what I will call "legacy management," that I have in mind when referring to the "social construction" of a political figure.

There is every good reason for those of us in the academy—we who have taken professional vows to devote ourselves to truth—to deplore this activity and to try to expose its distortions. (Regrettably, as matters turn out, many of the leading legacy managers in America happen themselves to be political scientists and historians who practice their counterfeit art under the cover of scholarly neutrality.) But if we take a step back and try to be analysts of the political process rather than judges or censures of our profession, candor obliges us to admit not only that legacy managers are here to stay but also that they play a large role in shaping political discussion in America. Legacy managers would not exist unless there was a market for their activity. This fact may not excuse them, but it at least makes what they do appear more understandable.

LEGACY MANAGERS AND THE BATTLE FOR POLITICAL IDEAS

Legacy management is limited to the cases of certain presidents. All presidents, of course, go down somewhere in history and end up being ranked by the community of historians and presidential scholars, and there will always be some people who have an interest in these judgments, foremost among whom are the presidents themselves, their families and friends, and the staff members employed at those mausoleums known as presidential libraries. Yet the truth is that beyond the time of their service in the White House and their final political campaign, most presidents are quickly forgotten, and their legacies have little or no political impact. Think, for example, of the cases of Chester Arthur and Gerald Ford. This result may be no reflection on such presidents' merits or contributions; it is just a simple fact of life. Legacy managers, as defined here, have no interest in such cases, and they will not be disturbed in the least if those making the judgments about these presidents happen to have a genuine regard for the truth.

Nor, at the opposite end of the spectrum, will the legacy manager be much concerned with those grand legacies of a select few presidents—Washington, Jefferson, and Lincoln—that hover far above the mundane preoccupations of ordinary partisan politics. These legacies touch in different ways on our general understanding of the meaning of America, and as such they remain of great interest to certain kinds of thinkers. It has been said of Jefferson, for example, that he has long been a kind of symbol, serving as "a sensitive reflector . . . of America's troubled search for the image of itself."[1] From this observation, the historian Gordon Wood has concluded that Jefferson "has become someone invented, manipulated, turned into something we Americans like or dislike."[2] It is almost as if Wood had used the word "constructed." But this kind of legacy controversy, though suggestive of the subject under consideration, no longer affects the concrete world of political influence or payoff.

Legacy managers in the strict sense get involved only in instances in which a legacy still counts as hard currency in the political marketplace, where it is "politically consequential." Legacies possessing this status are of different types. One type, which seeks to escape the bonds of partisanship, rests on evoking memories of a mood or feeling that was said to prevail under a particular president. The prime example is the Kennedy legacy, dubbed "Camelot" by some of its critics, which features warm images of youth, hope, and idealism. Few legacies have enjoyed a more skilled set of managers, among whom are included such luminaries as John Kenneth Galbraith, Arthur Schlesinger Jr., and Theodore Sorensen. All these men served with President Kennedy and continued for a long time thereafter to reap enormous dividends from the continuing warm glow of the Kennedy legacy. This legacy continues to exercise an effect. It was rolled out with much fanfare during the 2008 nomination process, when a good part of the Kennedy family endorsed Barack Obama, seeking to wrap the Kennedy mantle around him. Daughter Caroline argued that he would be able to make people "feel inspired and hopeful about America the way people did when my father was president."[3]

Another type of politically consequential legacy is of a "harder" or more partisan political sort. It derives from the reputation of the president's leadership skill and, especially, from the alleged merits of his public philosophy as shown by the concrete achievements it promoted. This type of legacy will usually be strongly contested—legacy managers will be at work on both sides—because the battle over political ideas may continue long after a president has left office.

WHAT MAKES A LEGACY CONSEQUENTIAL?

We thus arrive at the interesting question of why some legacies become politically consequential while others do not. No simple answer exists, but four conditions seem, at least in the case of the harder variant, to contribute to the result: first, when a president prominently sets forth a public philosophy and when the stakes that accompany its articulation are great; second, when partisans at the time view the stakes as great, voluntarily agreeing to a public test of the merits and worth of the new ideas; third, when there is something distinctive or controversial about the character of the president, giving the legacy controversy a "personal dimension"; and finally, when, after the president has served, significant parts of the elite determine that they want to keep the contest alive.

The case of Ronald Reagan, I believe, fulfills these four conditions more completely—not each individually, but all four together, as a kind of average—than does the case of any other president in American history. It is no accident, then, that controversy over his legacy has continued for so long. Reagan's "competitors" for the most politically consequential legacy during their respective historical times are Jefferson, Jackson, Lincoln, and FDR. When it comes to the magnitude of the actual stakes that were involved, more was at issue when Lincoln, FDR, and (perhaps) Jefferson came to power, but not Jackson. With Jefferson and Lincoln, however, large-scale political opposition collapsed in the immediate aftermath of their presidencies. The anti-Jefferson forces were confined to the rapidly fading Federalist Party, while public opposition to Lincoln was limited largely to southern whites. The result was that the fourth condition—a desire to keep the battle going—was not met in these instances in nearly the same degree as it has been in Reagan's case. FDR in this respect would be closer to Reagan, because the battle over the public philosophy of New Deal liberalism continued to be waged, at least in certain circles, for some time. But part of the ideological hostility to FDR was mollified by his wartime leadership, which was acknowledged across party lines. Reagan never had an occasion to achieve this kind of nonpartisan appeal.

When it comes to the third condition, the personal factor (especially in the form of negative portrayals by the opposition), all five of these presidents faced very significant attacks. Comparative judgments here are difficult, but an estimate can be hazarded that would place personal opposition to Reagan (a) "above" that encountered by Lincoln, who was attacked more for his ideas than his character; (b) on a par with that encountered by Jefferson and FDR, who were both highly mistrusted; and (c) below that endured by Andrew Jackson, who was probably the most vilified of all presidents. The legacy struggle over Jackson was intense and continued for almost two decades—a period that historians have dubbed the Age of Jackson—although it did not outlast the time that has already been clocked by the controversy over Ronald Reagan. Because of this fact alone, should not the current era be known as the Age of Reagan?

RONALD REAGAN'S LEGACY STRUGGLE

Quitting these historical speculations, let us turn directly to the case in question. The origin of the legacy struggle over Ronald Reagan lay in the 1980 presidential campaign. Reagan is one of only a few presidential candidates who, prior to his election, offered an important new public philosophy. He was nominated as the head of a popular movement that captured his party, a feat for which he was enthusiastically embraced by his core supporters. Ideologically, he stood far from the prevailing status quo, offering the American people what appeared to be a very clear choice.

Whatever might finally be said, however, about the actual magnitude of the change Reagan sought, there is no doubt about how his program was viewed by the participants at the time. Even more than his proponents, his opponents insisted on calling attention to the radical character of his philosophy. The intellectual elite of the Democratic Party missed no opportunity labeling his positions "extreme" and arguing that his thinking was primitive, simplistic, and atavistic. Policies based on conservative ideas, his critics insisted, would ruin the country and threaten peace and order in the world.

Opponents further upped the ante by adding a personal dimension to the contest. Ronald Reagan was said to be a fool or, in slightly nicer language (that of Clark Clifford), an "amiable dunce." Following the assassination attempt on him in 1981, when Reagan showed grace under fire, his personal popularity grew to such an extent that the most severe attacks on his character became ill advised, but the overall strategy of belittling his intelligence remained the same. One of the best expressions of this view—best because it sums up, with a surfeit of pretentiousness, what so many others were saying and thinking—came from the celebrated political scientist Michael Rogin, who argued that Reagan's real life philosophy derived from the movie scripts from his acting career. Reagan, the actor, could not tell the difference between reality and fiction, and he brought the same delusions, or illusions, into American politics.[4] (This period was still one in which liberals were sufficiently proud of their intellectual pedigree that they could take pleasure in expressing their contempt for Hollywood, in contrast to today, when many are wont to fawn over the intellectual acumen of the likes of an Alec Baldwin.)

The attacks on Reagan's policies did not abate with his accession to the presidency. His domestic plan to cut taxes and limit government spending brought a huge and hostile reaction. It was not long before someone—it is still not known whether it was a proponent or opponent—coined the term "Reagan revolution" to describe his program. The language in this case might have been a bit hyperbolic, but the elite of the Democratic Party embraced it, and the perception of what was at stake grew greater by the day. The debates in the following two years on questions of foreign policy were even more intense. Reagan's call for a defense buildup, his refusal to cede to the mass hysteria of the nuclear freeze movement, and his expressions of anti-Communism, culminating in his provocative identification of the Soviet Union as an "evil empire," led his opponents to label him an ideological extremist and a threat to world peace.

The upshot of these confrontations was that both sides entered into a solemn covenant, agreeing that Ronald Reagan's program and philosophy should be treated as the ultimate test about the way to govern. Thus by the end of his first term, the first three of the four conditions for a legacy controversy had been fully satisfied. The prospect of avoiding such a battle depended now on one side's deciding, after Reagan left office, to give up the fight.

PARADOX AND IRONY IN THE REAGAN LEGACY

Fast-forward now to 1990. Much happened in the decade that began with Ronald Reagan's election in 1980, but four developments—I will refer to them as the Big Four—stand out. All four, at first glance, seem to reflect well on Reagan's presidency, and three appear as huge benefits for the nation.

1. an end to the widespread view of the late 1960s and 1970s that the presidency was a broken institution and that the nation could not be governed;
2. the rise of conservatism as a major force in America, not only in the electoral realm but increasingly in the media and in the arena of the production and dissemination of ideas in public policy;
3. a major improvement of economic conditions as measured by almost all of the important macroeconomic indices; and
4. a complete transformation of the world order, marked by the end of the cold war, the collapse of Communism, the end of the Soviet empire, and the victory of the West.

Supporters of Ronald Reagan were naturally quick to cite these developments and assign much of the credit for them to the president. Their argument was that because these things began to happen during Reagan's tenure, and because Reagan was conspicuously involved in each of them, his leadership and policies were in a large degree responsible for what had taken place. Taking the argument a step further, his conservative philosophy, favoring market approaches and low taxes in domestic affairs and a strong defense and a staunch anti-Communist posture in foreign affairs, had been vindicated.

For Reagan's opponents, the Big Four presented an obvious challenge. To admit that these developments, particularly the last two, resulted from Ronald Reagan's leadership skill and governing philosophy would seem to concede too much: that liberals had lost their grand wager. Yet damaging as such a concession sounds, instances of standing down are not as rare as one might think, and democratic politics could not be conducted without them. Other parties on different occasions in American history have had to come to terms with performing this kind of unpleasant task. It is a matter of cutting losses and trying to move on. Nor is it really necessary to grant everything to the opposition or engage in public acts of penance. All that is needed is to artfully admit a large point or two and then do one's best to change the subject to matters where the opposition's record might be weaker.

There were some in the Democratic Party who counseled just such a strategy. But much of the party's liberal wing opted to fight on, adopting a scorched-earth policy of denying all credit to Ronald Reagan. This stance is what led to the fulfillment of the fourth and final condition for perpetuating a legacy war. Liberal managers deployed two general lines of arguments to cope with the Big Four. The first was to agree that certain positive things occurred but to insist that they took place not because of anything Ronald Reagan had done but because of luck or the good efforts of others, sometimes even in spite of Ronald Reagan's policies. The most notable application of this line of argument appeared in the analysis of foreign affairs, where the positive character of the events was clearest. A typical argument was that Reagan just happened to be in office when the moment arrived for the collapse of Communism. According to Raymond Moore, a noted expert on foreign affairs, "While some presidents are gifted in their conduct of foreign affairs, Reagan was lucky. . . . Reagan was a very fortunate president able to take advantage of forces and trends outside his control (and use them for his benefit)."[5]

At least this position acknowledged that Reagan used fortune to his advantage, which, when one thinks about it, is no small mark of a competent statesman. The more robust position adopted by liberal legacy managers was to attribute these events in large measure to human agency, but neither to anything done by Ronald Reagan nor, by extension, by anyone who shared Reagan's view of Communism, such as Margaret Thatcher and perhaps Pope John Paul II. All the credit instead went to the Soviet leader Mikhail Gorbachev, and not just to Mikhail Gorbachev but to Mikhail Gorbachev acting free of any pressures or inducements that derived from any of Ronald Reagan's policies. The apotheosis of Gorbachev, which reached the status of near idolatry, became the liberal legacy managers' main strategy for handling the "problem" of a positive assessment of Reagan's presidency.

Even this, however, did not go far enough for some. They took the next step of arguing that the fall of Communism actually confirmed the liberal understanding rather than the conservative one. Reagan's hard line made things much worse, and but for his policies, the wall would have come down faster. Liberal legacy managers cited with approval the view of the venerable George Kennan, who concluded that the "extreme militarization" pursued by Reagan "consistently strengthened comparable hard-liners in the Soviet Union." According to Strobe Talbott, "The Soviet system has gone into meltdown because of inadequacies and defects at its core, not because of anything the outside world has done or not done." In fact, Talbott went on, the collapse of the Soviet Union proved that the threat it posed was never as great as conservatives liked to make out: "The doves in the great debate of the past forty years were right all along."[6]

The more moderate Democrats, including many in the Democratic Leadership Council, such as Joseph Lieberman and Bill Clinton, saw the danger for the Democratic Party in the continuation of the full-scale legacy war against Ronald Reagan on this point. As early as 1991, Clinton signaled his readiness to have the Democratic Party move on and adopt another approach. He praised Reagan's "rhetoric in defense of freedom" and his role in "advancing the idea that communism could be rolled back." He continued, "The idea that we were going to stand firm and reaffirm our containment strategy, and the fact that we forced [the Soviets] to spend even more when they were already producing a Cadillac defense system and a dinosaur economy, I think it hastened their undoing."[7]

The second line of argument of liberal legacy managers was to contend that a result that seemed positive was so only on the surface. The good that people thought they saw under Reagan's presidency was cosmetic, representing a short-term fix at the expense of a real long-term solution, or it was accompanied by negative consequences that far outweighed in importance the positive ones. This approach served as the prime way to handle the "problem" of the economic recovery that took place in the 1980s.

After initially denying and belittling the notion that tax cuts could improve economic performance, liberals came around to the view that the real source of the economic improvement had been not the tax cuts but the huge budget deficits. The growth that was generated by this policy, dubbed "Reaganomics," was not only unsustainable but spurious. It was based on placing the real costs on the backs of future generations, which would have to pay for the current generation's profligacy. Haynes Johnson called the 1980s "an age of illusion when America lived on borrowed time."[8] The more interesting critique, however, was one that contended that even if an economic recovery had taken place, it was produced at the cost of a profound moral deterioration. The 1980s was "a decade of greed." This phrase, which played on some of the spectacular excesses of this period of rapid growth, was meant to deny the substantiality of the development that had occurred. The wealth that was generated was ill gotten and went to the richest and most rapacious, not to the average American.

The high (or low) point of the effort of liberal legacy managers to discredit the Reagan presidency appeared (or was reflected) in a poll of selected presidential scholars, mostly historians, that was taken in 1996, for the purpose of ranking American presidents. The scholars, persons generally of much distinction, judged Reagan to be an utter mediocrity, just above the insignificant Chester Arthur and the hapless Jimmy Carter.[9] The specific grounds for the scholars' judgment are not known. Given that many, though not all of them, were liberal, it is quite likely that they would have found fault with many of Reagan's actions and policies in areas beyond the Big Four noted here, including Reagan's judicial appointments and his stance on questions of civil rights. And they certainly could have found grounds for doubting Reagan's grasp on the presidency as a result of the grave problems of management in the Iran-contra affair.

Yet even if one gives full weight to all of these objections, one would still have to figure that, as historians, these scholars would judge matters in the broad sweep of time and according to the big picture. Under such a view—provided Reagan could be given at least some credit for the Big Four—it would be impossible to judge him mediocre; he would have to be considered estimable. Only two possible explanations can therefore account for their assessment: either these historians descended, in this instance, into liberal legacy managers, abusing their academic credentials to engage in a purely political act, or they were convinced by the arguments of the other liberal legacy managers that the positive things that took place during Reagan's presidency were not of his doing or were spurious. As I find it inconceivable to accept the first possibility (that they behaved dishonorably), I am forced to adopt the second (that they succumbed to the manipulation of legacy managers).

Why did the Left insist on unleashing its legacy managers to undermine Ronald Reagan, when a different policy seems to have been more in the interest of the Democratic Party? There are two plausible explanations, one rational and the other psychological. The rational explanation has to do with the bitter struggles that had been going on among factions within the Democratic Party. The Left faction on foreign policy, dating back to its opposition to the Vietnam War, had so invested in its criticism of the military and of staunch anti-Communism that it could not make any concession on this point without relinquishing its control of the Democratic Party. If it had been otherwise, there would have been no reason that Democrats could not have taken a different path and claimed that the hard-line position against Communism had been the policy of both parties (as indeed it once had been) and that both parties could therefore share the credit for the triumph. By attacking Reagan and conservatism, they foreclosed this option and chose to give all the credit to Gorbachev rather than to the positions of Harry Truman, John Kennedy, and former senators such as Henry Jackson.

Beyond this rational political calculation, however, there is an important psychological explanation for why the Left continued the attack on Ronald Reagan. The intellectual elite in America, up through the end of the 1990s, simply did not respect its opposition. Thinkers on the left had so dominated intellectual discourse for the previous half century that their notions of what was an intellectual and what was thinking could not allow for treating conservatism seriously. It was not that conservative arguments were wrong; it was that they were not arguments at all. The notion of Ronald Reagan's being just an actor, a dunce, was at once a reflection and a confirmation of this view. Reagan could not have been giving voice to an alternative intellectual position, because such a position simply did not exist. To cede in the face of another argument was difficult enough, but to cede to no thought at all was more than the liberal intellectuals' pride could bear.

The contest over Ronald Reagan's legacy continued unabated throughout the 1990s. The positive image was currency of the most valuable sort among Republicans and for George W. Bush in 2000, who managed to strike many in the party as the little Gipper. For the left, the effort to discredit Reagan continued. But sometime around the turn of the century, the tide began to turn, if not with the most inveterate of liberal partisans then with a broad spectrum of the American people and, eventually, with the majority of the scholarly community. Behind this change lay the efforts of many of the real biographers, who presented certain facts in a way that confounded the efforts of the best legacy managers to "construct" a Ronald Reagan to fit their ideology. These facts made clear that Ronald Reagan's interest and training in Hollywood were far more political in character than many had thought; that, in the years between acting and running for governor of California, he had spent an enormous amount of time, unprecedented for a modern political leader, reading, reflecting, and sharpening his political arguments; and finally that leaders of the Soviet Union themselves acknowledged in their private deliberations that the Reagan defense buildup and hard line definitely influenced their actions and weakened their will. In the end, it turns out, "social construction" can go only so far.

NOTES

1. Merrill D. Peterson, *The Jefferson Image in the American Mind* (New York: Oxford University Press, 1960), 234.

2. Gordon S. Wood, *Revolutionary Characters: What Made the Founders Different* (New York: Penguin Press, 2006), 94.

3. Caroline Kennedy, "A President like My Father," *New York Times*, January 27, 2008.

4. Michael Paul Rogin, *Ronald Reagan, the Movie and Other Episodes in Political Demonology* (Berkeley: University of California Press, 1987).

5. Raymond Moore, "The Reagan Presidency and Foreign Policy," in *The Reagan Presidency: An Incomplete Revolution?* ed. Dilys M. Hill, Raymond A. Moore, and Phil Williams (New York: St. Martin's Press, 1990), 197.

6. Kennan and Talbott quoted in Dinesh D'Souza, "How Reagan Won the Cold War," *National Review*, November 24, 1997, republished in *National Review Online*, June 6, 2004, http://www.nationalreview.com/flashback/dsouza200406061619.asp.

7. Clinton quoted in E. J. Dionne, "Clinton's Depressing Assault on Obama," *Washington Post,* January 25, 2008.

8. Haynes Johnson, *Sleepwalking through History: America in the Reagan Years* (New York: Norton, 1991), 13.

9. Arthur Schlesinger Jr., "The Ultimate Approval Rating," *New York Times Magazine,* December 15, 1996, 46–51; Arthur Schlesinger Jr., "Rating the Presidents: Washington to Clinton," *Political Science Quarterly* 112 (Summer 1997): 179–90.

Ronald Reagan's Legacy and American Conservatism

George H. Nash

In 2008, a specter haunted American politics: the genial specter of Ronald Reagan. More than any of our other presidents—more even than the incumbent at the time—Reagan was on the minds and tongues of a nation hungering for renewal. On the Republican side, presidential candidates invoked his name daily as they vied to be perceived as his political heir. On the Democratic side, pundits speculated whether Barack Obama, with his oratorical skills, might just be a liberal Reagan. On television, on the radio, and in the blogosphere, conservative commentators extolled his legacy and asked, What would Reagan do if he were living today?

The phenomenal wave of interest in Ronald Reagan is a powerful reminder of his continuing influence on American life. Twenty years after he left the presidency, and fifteen years after he withdrew into the solitude of his final illness, he continues to shape the political identity of a large sector of the American electorate. It is not the least of his legacies to his country.

THE RISING TIDE OF PRESIDENTIAL LEGACIES

Legacy: how often we now hear this word when we think about our presidents. No longer do our chief executives confine themselves, while in office, to performing their constitutional duties. Instead—or so the media tell us—toward the end of their tenure they become preoccupied with seeking the plaudits of posterity. Thus in 2007, more than an entire year before President George W. Bush was to leave office, the media began to assure us that he would be devoting his remaining days in the White House to creating a "legacy."[1]

The urge to build a legacy (and thereby, presumably, impress future historians) does not diminish when a president walks out of the Oval Office for the last time. One of the interesting phenomena in American politics in the past half century has been the invention and institutionalization of the hyperactive ex-presidency, dedicated in part to enhancing a president's reputation beyond his term of office and even beyond the grave. Our first modern ex-president was the energetic Theodore Roosevelt, who was only fifty years old when he left the White House in 1909. Unlike most of his successors, Roosevelt did not focus much on long-term legacy building, perhaps because he spent so much of his time trying to become president again. A more representative figure —and arguably the true inventor of the ex-presidency—was Herbert Hoover, who left office in 1933 and lived for another thirty-one and a half years, making him the longest-serving former president in our history. Hoover did many things in those years, but one theme was paramount: his unflagging desire to vindicate his record in the eyes of his contemporaries, as well as of generations to come.

Now if one were to ask leading politicians (such as presidents) to ruminate about their future place in history books, most would probably profess to be unconcerned (no doubt because it could appear egotistical to openly admit otherwise). George W. Bush, for instance, seems nonchalant about the subject. He has pointed out with jocularity that historians are still analyzing the presidencies of George Washington and Abraham Lincoln. He has remarked that he "will be long gone before the true history of the Bush administration is written."[2] He has even suggested that it would be an act of dishonor for him to use his power to try to inflate his stock among future historians. "You betray the office," he says, "if you get caught up" in "your personal standing."[3]

If Bush seems unworried about what scholars will someday say about him, few of our nation's chief executives behave this way anymore. No longer do our presidents leave their presidencies alone when they vacate the White House. Instead, they create presidential libraries, museums, and public policy centers to present their stories to the public. They publish memoirs big enough to be doorstops. Their closest associates produce a barrage of memoirs of their own, sometimes even before the presidents leave power. Out in the country, groups of admirers organize to preserve historically significant sites associated with the lives of the great men.

Increasingly, Congress chimes in with honorific initiatives of its own. In 1975, for instance, three years after the death of former president Truman, Congress created an official federal memorial to him to be known as the Harry S. Truman Scholarship Foundation, which to this day awards federally funded scholarships to college students intending to pursue careers in public service. In 1978 Congress established a federal memorial for Herbert Hoover, in the form of an additional building for the Hoover Institution at Stanford University. The Woodrow Wilson International Center for Scholars in Washington DC has become the federal memorial to our twenty-eighth president. And so it goes.

The impulse to memorialize our presidents has even begun to extend to presidential candidates who never got to be president at all. The Hubert H. Humphrey Fellowship Program (announced by President Carter in 1978), the Barry M. Goldwater Scholarship and Excellence in Education Program (created by Congress in 1986), and the Robert J. Dole Institute of Politics at the University of Kansas come to mind. One catalyst for these ventures has undoubtedly been the example of the most famous public policy enterprise of all: the Harvard University Institute of Politics, which the Kennedy family and its friends established in the 1960s, not long after the assassination of JFK.

Increasingly, then, the history of the American presidency is not simply what historians and other academic scribblers say it is, at least not in the short run. Instead, the interpretation of a president's legacy has become a deliberate and organized undertaking, involving the former president himself.

Creating the Reagan Legacy

The career of Ronald Reagan has not been exempt from this process. Like every one of his predecessors since Herbert Hoover,[4] Reagan created a presidential library and museum for his papers after he left office. In 1990 he duly published a monumental, 746-page autobiography.[5] Since the 1980s, members of his presidential team—from cabinet officers to speechwriters, from pollsters and personal staff to ambassadors and the First Lady herself—have generated a torrent of fascinating memoirs, probably the largest and richest such trove for any president in our history. From his boyhood home in Dixon, Illinois, to his magnificent ranch near Santa Barbara, California, important parts of Reagan's "landscape" have been preserved for the edification of future generations.

Yet in one respect Reagan was decisively different from most of his immediate predecessors and successors: except for creating a presidential library, and the nearly obligatory memoir to go along with it, Reagan did little to define and refine his legacy after he left the White House. Partly this was because of his advancing age: he was nearly seventy-eight years old (and by far the oldest of any of our presidents) when he left Washington in 1989, and he was truly ready to retire. What is sadder, the onset of Alzheimer's disease in 1994 deprived him of any further opportunity—even if he had desired one—to remain on the public stage and try to influence the verdict of history. Most important, Reagan made little further effort to furbish his legacy because, at bottom, he felt no need to do so. He was genuinely content with most of his record at the nation's helm.

Consider his televised farewell address to the American people in early 1989, in which he acclaimed his beloved country (as he had so often) as a "shining city upon a hill," blessed by God and chosen by him for a noble purpose. "And how stands the city on this winter night?" Reagan asked. "More prosperous, more secure, and happier than it was eight years ago . . . still a beacon, still a magnet for all who must have freedom." To "the men and women of the Reagan revolution," he said, "My friends: we did it. We weren't just marking time. We made a difference. We made the city stronger, we made the city freer, and we left her in good hands. All in all, not bad, not bad at all."[6]

Unlike such presidents as Herbert Hoover, Richard Nixon, Jimmy Carter, and Bill Clinton, Reagan felt no compulsion to "run for ex-president" or to seek exoneration in the eyes of history. His legacy seemed to him plain enough, and it needed no defense.

But if Reagan himself seemed serene about his accomplishments, many of his ardent admirers were less so—and less inclined to let the judgment of history take its course. In 1997 the conservative activist Grover Norquist and his Americans for Tax Reform organization launched a bold and unprecedented initiative known as the Reagan Legacy Project. Its stated objective was to honor Reagan's legacy by naming "significant public landmarks" after him in every state of the union as well as in more than three thousand counties throughout the United States. In 1998 the project's organizers succeeded in having Washington DC's National Airport officially renamed the Ronald Reagan Washington National Airport. It was the first of a number of such victories in the politics of memory.[7] Nor was this all. Since the 1990s there has been talk on the right about adding Reagan's countenance to Mount Rushmore (much to the annoyance and trepidation of some American liberals). More recently, the conservative Heritage Foundation—the intellectual nerve center of the Reagan revolution during the 1980s—inaugurated a yearlong campaign of political education on the radio and the Internet. Its arresting title: "What Would Reagan Do?"[8]

Clearly the nation's fortieth president continues to appeal to the American imagination—and not just to his own devoted partisans. Type in the words "Reagan biography" at Amazon.com; one will discover more than 850 listed items. Or conduct an Internet search for the exact phrase "Reagan legacy"; more than 800,000 results will appear.[9] Or consult the Ronald Reagan Presidential Foundation's latest catalogue. In its thirty-two pages, one will find available for purchase Reagan books, neckties, posters, CDs, DVDs, medallions, and much else.

To some scoffers the groundswell of "Reagan nostalgia" (as they dismissively call it) is little more than a right-wing equivalent of the liberal cult of John F. Kennedy's Camelot. But what is most noteworthy about this phenomenon is not its occasionally nostalgic trimmings but its unabashedly pedagogical motivation. Each year, for example, the conservative Young America's Foundation brings thousands of college and high school students to its Reagan Ranch Center in Santa Barbara, California, and to the nearby Reagan ranch itself (which the foundation now owns). There it holds numerous lectures and classes on Reagan's life and philosophy, events often carried on C-SPAN. The foundation proudly styles its Santa Barbara facility as a "Schoolhouse for Reaganism" and includes members of his administration on its Reagan Ranch board of directors. Similarly, the Heritage Foundation's "What Would Reagan Do?" project, initiated in early 2008, proclaims him a "role model" for present and future political leaders. Why? In the words of the foundation's president, Edwin J. Feulner, Reagan was politically successful "because he spoke powerfully to the American people about conservative principles—which he would not compromise!"[10]

What is one to make of this enduring fascination with America's fortieth president? Obviously the mood of the moment has something to do with it: in 2008 the political coalition that Reagan forged was widely perceived to be in disarray, and memories of the Gipper reminded embattled conservatives of better days. But current events do not fully explain a phenomenon that has been building for nearly twenty years. We must probe more deeply. Why has the celebration of Reagan's legacy become a "project"? Why the fervent determination to preserve, protect, and defend the historical reputation of this man?

CONSERVATISM AND THE REAGAN LEGACY

To answer these questions, we must understand Ronald Reagan's special relationship with modern American conservatism.

Reagan was a conservative politician, of course, but there were many others during his long career, and he was by no means the most militant among them. When he ran for president in 1980, he was not even the sole conservative in the field. (Representative Philip Crane of Illinois was also a contender.) Reagan was articulate, but so were Barry Goldwater and Robert Taft. Unlike them, he succeeded in becoming president, but so, too, did several other Republicans during his lifetime. Yet it was Reagan who became the most revered conservative leader since Calvin Coolidge. Why?

Obviously his personal charm, wit, optimistic temperament, transparent decency, authoritative physical appearance, and oratorical talent were tremendous assets. Someone said of him that he "could get a standing ovation in a graveyard."[11] He was, in that now hackneyed phrase, the Great Communicator. His sense of humor and gifts as a raconteur were legendary; not surprisingly, entire anthologies of his witticisms and stories are now in print. Thanks in large measure to Reagan, a healthy sense of humor is an attribute we now hope to find in our chief executives. Indeed, one of his subtle legacies has been what one might call the theatrical presidency: the public expectation that our presidents will in some sense entertain us even as they govern.

But Reagan's personal qualities do not definitively explain his profound appeal to the American Right. John F. Kennedy was another witty and charismatic president and no slouch as a speaker, but he was never a favorite of the nation's conservatives. Reagan gained their favor not so much because of his winsome personality and superlative communication skills but because they liked and believed what he said. His message was more important than the messenger.[12]

But even this observation does not completely hit the mark. Other contemporary politicians "talked the talk" just as sincerely as Reagan did, but he—not they—won the conservatives' fealty and affection. The question persists, Why was he different?

First, unlike most of the Republican politicians of his day, Reagan was something of an intellectual: a man who not only spoke the language of the Right but seriously thought about it. He was, we now know, an inveterate and voracious reader of conservative literature, including Whittaker Chambers's classic anti-Communist autobiography *Witness*, which influenced him hugely (and parts of which he committed to memory).[13] More likely than not, he read Friedrich Hayek's *The Road to Serfdom* (1944) and Henry Hazlitt's *Economics in One Lesson* (1946), two of the foundational texts of free-market philosophy after World War II. As a spokesman for General Electric between 1954 and 1962, Reagan was exposed to the cascade of libertarian, limited government, antisocialist publications that the company relentlessly disseminated to its employees. The company's brilliant public relations strategist, Lemuel Boulware, became a lifelong friend. Reagan himself referred to his work at GE as "almost a postgraduate course in political science for me."[14] Thanks perhaps to Boulware, Reagan became an early and lifelong reader of William F. Buckley Jr.'s *National Review* (founded in 1955), which he came to regard and publicly acknowledge as his "favorite magazine."[15] He also avidly read the influential conservative weekly *Human Events* and often clipped articles from its pages.[16]

In the 1950s, in short, Reagan became—and remained ever after—a conservative by conviction, not convenience. He consumed books and tracts of the Right with zest, and he believed.

Second, and again unlike most Republican presidential aspirants of his era, Reagan was what activists on the right call a "movement conservative": one who associated himself not merely with a few conservative causes and catchwords but with the intellectuals, journalists, and public policy entrepreneurs who were steadfastly building a movement of ideas. Richard Nixon, by contrast, seemed to regard conservatives as a prickly interest group, to be handled gingerly and appeased. Reagan did infinitely more, and conservatives noticed.

Both before and during his presidency, Reagan displayed his affinity for the conservative movement in a multitude of ways. He joined the national advisory board of the conservative youth organization Young Americans for Freedom. In 1984 he awarded the Presidential Medal of Freedom posthumously to Whittaker Chambers, one of the conservative icons of the cold war. It was an action keenly appreciated on the right. In 1988 he conferred the same high honor on the free-market economist Milton Friedman. Two months later he gave a Presidential Citizens Medal to the distinguished conservative scholar Russell Kirk. Reagan was the featured speaker at *National Review*'s thirtieth anniversary gala in 1985 and at the Heritage Foundation's anniversary banquet in 1986. More telling still, on eight separate occasions during his presidency, he addressed in person the annual Conservative Political Action Conference in Washington DC: a giant gathering of the faithful from all across the land. And he instituted the custom of annually addressing his administration's political appointees at a pep rally held each January in the nation's capital. He never forgot that he represented a political and intellectual movement, and he repeatedly let its leaders know that he considered himself to be one of their tribe. Many of his gestures were symbolic, to be sure, but in politics, as in marriage, little things mean a lot.

And here we come to the third reason for Reagan's extraordinary bond with his fellow conservatives. Before 1980, the conservative insurgency since World War II had been largely an alliance of dissenters, outside the American political mainstream looking in. When Reagan won the presidency that year, he scored more than a smashing personal victory; he brought American conservatives into the promised land inside the Beltway. He conferred prestige on them and legitimized them as players in the political big leagues. He secured for them a permanent beachhead in the epicenter of national politics, and they were grateful.

In assessing Reagan's legacy for conservatives, it is important to remember that the movement that came to power with him was not a monolith. It was a coalition of five distinct parts:

1. classical liberals and libertarians, apprehensive of the threat of overweening government and the welfare state to individual liberty and free-market capitalism;
2. "traditionalist" conservatives, appalled by the weakening of the ethical norms and institutional foundations of American society at the hands of secular, relativistic liberalism;

3. anti-Communist cold warriors, convinced that America was increasingly imperiled by an evil empire seeking the conquest of the world;

4. neoconservatives—disillusioned men and women of the Left who had been "mugged by reality" and were gravitating toward the conservative camp; and

5. the Religious Right, traumatized by the moral wreckage unleashed on America by the courts and by the culture wars of the 1960s and 1970s.

Reagan himself seems to have been closest in his outlook and priorities to the free-market conservatives and cold warriors. In his first autobiography, published in 1965, he asserted that classical liberalism was "now the conservative position."[17] On another occasion he declared, "Today's conservative is, of course, the true liberal—in the classical meaning of the word."[18] But the president was astute enough to identify himself (and sincerely so) with each component of the grand coalition. To a convention of fifteen thousand evangelical Christians in 1980, for instance, he famously remarked, "I know you can't endorse me. But I want you to know that I endorse you."[19] It could even be said that Reagan was a premature neoconservative, for he had once been a very liberal Democrat. Just after the election of 1980, he warmly endorsed a new book on foreign policy by the neoconservative writer Norman Podhoretz.[20]

Thus, just as William F. Buckley Jr. had done for conservatives out of power before 1980, Reagan as president during the 1980s performed an emblematic and ecumenical function. Much of his popularity as a conservative paladin derived from his ability to embody all these impulses simultaneously.

Yet Reagan did more than simply give his fellow conservatives access to power. He also placed his own distinctive brand on their movement—thereby cementing the bond between them. At the time of his accession to the presidency, the American Right was completing a transition from a dissident, minority consciousness to a perception of itself as the authentic voice of middle America. Once upon a time, during the 1950s, many conservatives had gloomily regarded themselves as a forlorn and defeated remnant, "standing athwart history, yelling Stop!"[21] By 1980 they had begun to speak of themselves in more populist terms, as the vanguard of America's silent, moral majority.

Reagan's electoral triumph completed this mainstreaming process. More than that, he imbued it with rhetorical staying power. As Michael Barone has observed, the Great Communicator gave American conservatism a demotic voice and a more optimistic tone, evoking hope for the future instead of nostalgia for a receding past. Unlike some of the more European-oriented conservative intellectuals, he couched his social vision in the language of American exceptionalism, the lilting religious imagery of America as a chosen nation, chosen by God "to be free" and to be "the golden hope of all mankind." He believed this. He believed, too, in words of Tom Paine, which he loved to quote: "We have it in our power to begin the world over again."[22]

So in his inaugural address in 1981, Reagan exhorted his fellow citizens "to believe in ourselves and to believe in our capacity to perform great deeds."[23] His invincible optimism, his unquenchable confidence in the elixir of freedom, his conviction that history is not predetermined, inspired not only Americans in general but a generation of his fellow conservatives.

All this is not to say that American conservatives were enraptured by Reagan's performance in the presidency. Truth to tell, they were often dismayed and disappointed, although more by his advisers than by the man himself. In our current mood of celebration of Reagan's legacy, we tend to forget what contemporary observers and the burgeoning memoir literature about him attest: that in both the domestic and foreign policy arenas, the Reagan administration was often at war with itself. It was a war, as the expression of the time had it, between pragmatists and ideologues—that is, between middle-of-the-road, pre-Reaganite Republicans and principled "movement conservatives" intent on effecting a revolution. The conflict permeated the highest levels of the White House staff, involved the president's wife (who sided with the pragmatists), and engendered internecine feuds and manipulative policy-making processes that aptly have been described as byzantine. It gave rise to the great conservative battle cry of the 1980s: "Let Reagan be Reagan."

Particularly during the president's second term, his increasingly intensive pursuit of arms control agreements with the Soviet Union offended and alarmed many conservatives, both inside and outside his administration. Especially perturbed was the neoconservative journal *Commentary*, edited by Norman Podhoretz, which published a number of highly critical articles on this subject during the mid- and late

1980s.[24] Reagan's zealous drive for the total abolition of nuclear weapons—culminating in the roller-coaster summit conference in Reykjavik in 1986—made even Margaret Thatcher fear that he had gone wobbly.[25] On the whole, it is safe to say that Reagan's first term was more congenial to conservatives than his second.

When Reagan left the White House in 1989, not everyone on the right was ready to give him a grade of A. Libertarians, especially, wondered just how much had really been accomplished during his two terms. One prominent libertarian—dismayed by the administration's perceived inability (or unwillingness) "to reverse the growth of Leviathan"—published an essay provocatively titled "The Sad Legacy of Ronald Reagan."[26] Nevertheless, most movement conservatives credited Reagan with bequeathing them a politically precious gift—a successful, conservative presidency—and their verdict was accordingly positive.[27] So, too, was that of most other Americans: in January 1989, Reagan left office with a public approval rating of well over 60 percent—the highest for any departing president since Franklin Roosevelt.

The "shining city upon a hill," it seemed, had been well served. The looming question for conservatives was, Would historians agree?

HISTORIANS AND THE REAGAN LEGACY

According to a historian of my acquaintance, scholarly appraisals of a president's legacy go through three stages: bunk, debunk, and rebunk. At the beginning of 1989, there was reason to believe that the coming historical evaluation of Reagan's presidency would skip the first phase and permanently wallow in the second. Politicians often like to say that they will let history determine the merits of their record, as if history were a disembodied, infallible force. What more sophisticated politicians realize is that historical judgment is an artifact, the product of creatures known as historians who are not as free from bias as they like to think.

In the case of Ronald Reagan, this posed an immediate challenge. Despite his popularity with the general electorate at the end of his second term, there was one influential corner of America where he remained anathema: academe. For all of Reagan's wit, charm, and persuasiveness, his had been a highly polarizing presidency, and few academic social scientists inhabited his side of the great divide. Reagan was an unabashed conservative. The vast majority of historians and political scientists were not.

Not surprisingly, then, the leftward-tilting American intelligentsia in the 1980s largely looked on the president as at worst a warmonger and at best (in Clark Clifford's notorious phrase) as an "amiable dunce." The septuagenarian president was pilloried by Haynes Johnson as an indolent actor "sleepwalking through history." The contempt which many academics felt for him was captured in the response by the historian Henry Steele Commager to Reagan's 1983 address labeling the Soviet Union an "evil empire"—a speech roundly applauded by conservatives. According to the very liberal Commager, it was "the worst presidential speech in American history, and I've read them all."[28]

Reagan himself did not seem to mind the aspersions cast on him by his ideological enemies. As various biographers have noted, he always cared more about the "box office" (the voters) than about the critics. He also enjoyed letting his opponents underestimate him and seemed to play along with some of their misperceptions of his temperament. "It's true hard work never killed anybody," he once reputedly remarked, "but I figure, why take the chance."[29] On his desk in the White House, he kept a plaque that said, "There's no limit to what a man can do or where he can go if he doesn't mind who gets the credit." Still, the disdain that many in the professoriate expressed for him (and, even more, for his conservative political philosophy) made it seem unlikely that he would be treated favorably in the history books anytime soon.

The first scholarly evaluations of Reagan after he left the White House seemed to confirm his conservative defenders' worst fears. In 1990 the Siena Research Institute asked more than two hundred academic historians and political scientists to rank all forty American presidents. Reagan came in at an undistinguished twenty-second, just two notches ahead of Jimmy Carter. Four years later the institute conducted another survey; this time Reagan inched up to twenty—four places lower than the current incumbent, Bill Clinton.[30] In 1996 the liberal historian Arthur Schlesinger Jr. asked thirty prominent historians (and two Democratic politicians) to rank the presidents anew. Although seven accorded Reagan a "near great" ranking, nine others dismissed him as "below average," and four judged him an outright "failure." In the composite ranking, Reagan placed a mediocre twenty-fifth, just behind his successor in office, George H. W. Bush, and barely ahead of Chester Arthur.[31]

Schlesinger's poll outraged American conservatives. Nearly every participant in his survey was a left-of-center intellectual like him; only one of the thirty-two was a known conservative. Was this, conservatives wondered, how the "impartial" judgment of history would be rendered on Reagan? Perhaps not coincidentally, several months later, Grover Norquist initiated the Reagan Legacy Project. In the next several years, conservatively inclined presidential scholars came forth with rejoinders and correctives to Schlesinger, including *Presidential Leadership: Rating the Best and the Worst in the White House*.[32] In this volume, a more ideologically diverse set of academic experts moved Reagan into the "near great" category.

In retrospect, Schlesinger's skewed 1996 survey may be seen as the last hurrah of the anti-Reagan consensus in liberal academe. Shortly afterward, a funny thing happened on Reagan's journey into the history books: his reputation among professors began to rise. Here and there, reputable scholars—hardly any of them on the political right—began to publish books and articles containing more than a modicum of praise.[33] One sign of this new glasnost appeared in a 1999 essay in the *Washington Post* by the liberal political scientist and biographer of Franklin Roosevelt, James MacGregor Burns. "When historians tally up the [twentieth] century's 'great' or 'near-great' presidents," he declared flatly, "Roosevelt and Reagan will be among them."[34] It was a remarkable accolade, particularly considering its source.

Why this rapid shifting of the tide? Every president's place in history depends to some degree on the record of his immediate successors, and here Reagan was singularly fortunate. After the brief economic recession of 1991–1992, the economic revival that had commenced on his watch resumed: the long prosperity (it has been called), arguably rooted in the policies Reagan implemented in the early 1980s. One of the principal criticisms of Reagan had been that "Reaganomics" had led to huge and dangerous federal budget deficits. When the economy nevertheless grew stronger and the deficits disappeared in the 1990s, this part of Reagan's legacy came to seem far less consequential than once feared, and his free-market, low-tax philosophy seemed vindicated. The Republican capture of Congress in 1994 (including the House of Representatives for the first time in fifty-two years) ratified the Reagan revolution even further. Soon Bill Clinton himself was claiming that "the era of big government is over." Like the Labour Party leader Tony Blair after the "Thatcher revolution" in Great Britain during the 1980s, Clinton appeared to recognize that Reagan had pulled the political center of gravity to the right. That is one way to measure a presidential legacy.

Reagan's genuine likeability and his courageous response to Alzheimer's disease no doubt helped to dissipate some of the lingering hostility evinced by his ideological foes. His unruffled affability and dignified demeanor as chief executive contrasted favorably with the scandals and hyperpartisanship of the Clinton years (and beyond). But most of all, Reagan's reputation—and the new respect for his legacy—profited from the amazing events that occurred shortly after he left office: the liberation of Eastern Europe from Communist captivity and the collapse of the USSR just two years later.

With the advantage of hindsight, we tend to forget that it was not at all obvious on January 20, 1989—the day the Reagan administration officially ended—that the end of the Soviet empire was near. Reagan, of course, had publicly prophesied Communism's early demise.[35] But even he was surprised when the Berlin Wall came down less than ten months after he left office.[36] This swift and stunning geopolitical earthquake, and the attendant end of the cold war, confronted historians on the left and right with a monumental explanatory problem: How and why did all this happen, and so unexpectedly? Who was responsible? Who deserved credit? As the scholarly investigations proceeded, nearly every serious academic investigator came to recognize that Reagan's role in these shattering developments had been substantial.

To be sure, there were—and remain—sharp differences of emphasis among the scholars. In one corner stands the "Reagan victory school," which argues essentially that Reagan won the cold war, that he intended to win it, and that as president he conceived and carried out a coordinated campaign to achieve this objective.[37] In another corner are those who emphasize internal Soviet conditions and decision making, the pivotal role of Mikhail Gorbachev, and Reagan's pursuit of nuclear disarmament (over the objection of his more conservative advisers). The debate between these two schools is likely to continue at least until more of the Soviet archives are opened. But even the academic disparagers of Reaganite "triumphalism" seem inclined to grant that the Gipper was at the very least the "best supporting actor" in Gorbachev's drama and that Reagan's policies helped to push the Soviet Union toward irreversible reform.[38] Some would go further. There is no better example of

Reagan's change of fortune in academic scholarship than the judgment pronounced in 2004 by the dean of America's diplomatic historians, John Lewis Gaddis of Yale University. In his considered opinion, Reagan should be remembered as a highly skilled and effective geopolitician—indeed, as the most successful American strategist of the cold war.[39]

If events after 1989 encouraged a fresh and favorable interpretation of Reagan's legacy, another development proved nearly as important. Sooner or later, historical scholarship must be grounded not on the quicksand of political or academic fashion but on the solid bedrock of archival research. In the case of Reagan, the archival record turned out to be more effulgent than anyone dreamed.

Early in 2001 three scholars—Kiron Skinner, Martin Anderson, and Annelise Anderson—published a remarkable book of Reagan's own writings drawn from a previously unknown file in his personal papers.[40] Between 1975 and 1979, Reagan had delivered more than 1,000 daily syndicated radio broadcasts, each about five hundred words long, on nearly every public policy issue and controversy imaginable. It turned out that he composed 670 of these essays by himself, in his own handwriting, and that he personally edited them as well. A large sampling from this cache of primary sources composed the bulk of the volume *Reagan, in His Own Hand,* which Skinner and the Andersons assembled. It revealed a dimension of Reagan hitherto hidden from view. In 2003 the three scholars published an equally impressive sequel, *Reagan: A Life in Letters,* a compendium of more than one thousand substantive letters—entirely written by Reagan himself—out of an estimated ten thousand such letters that he is believed to have composed during his long life.

More than any other scholarly publications in the past twenty years, these anthologies demolished the old, demeaning stereotypes and propelled the upward arc of Reagan's reputation. The nation's fortieth president stood revealed as a prolific and capable writer, a skillful editor, a disciplined worker, a wide-ranging reader, and an intelligent, even visionary, thinker. Before his presidency, he wrote nearly all of his own speeches—a notable accomplishment in itself. Even in the White House, he drafted many of his major addresses himself and carefully edited his speechwriters' submissions. This was not the Reagan that his detractors (and even some admirers) thought they knew.

The surge of scholarly reappraisal was now approaching high tide.

In 2004 Paul Kengor published *God and Ronald Reagan,* a "spiritual bi-ography" that argued that in Reagan's religion lay the key to his character and much of his conduct as president. Far from being a merely nominal Christian, Reagan (in Kengor's account) was a deeply committed, if self-effacing, man of faith who was convinced that Gold had a plan—indeed, a mission—not only for America as a nation but for him as its president. According to Kengor, Reagan came to believe that God's purpose for him was to confront and defeat atheistic Communism.

Just how Reagan fulfilled this mission Kengor explained in his next book, *The Crusader: Ronald Reagan and the Fall of Communism.* Here Kengor portrayed Reagan as a man with a "sense of destiny" who sought to become president for a specific purpose: to effect the collapse of Communism and the breakup of its evil empire. Once in power, Reagan (claimed Kengor) pursued this goal relentlessly to victory.

Meanwhile, in 2005, Paul Lettow published a monograph, *Ronald Reagan and His Quest to Abolish Nuclear Weapons,* which illuminated an even less familiar part of Reagan's psyche: his lifelong loathing of nu-clear weapons and his growing determination as president to rid them from the earth. It seemed that Reagan was not only a cold warrior but also a nuclear abolitionist who "was convinced that it was his personal mission to avert nuclear war."[41]

In 2007 Reagan scholarship took another leap forward with the publication of his presidential diary, which he faithfully kept between 1981 and 1989.[42] Although this much-awaited tome yielded no spec-tacular revelations, it enhanced Reagan's stature as a genuinely decent person and reinforced the growing sense among scholars that he had been an astute and competent chief executive.

By the beginning of 2008, Reagan's historical reputation had soared to heights that few conservatives had thought attainable. It was now commonplace for academics and media commentators alike to acclaim him as one of America's most successful presidents. The new consensus did not mean that scholars agreed on what it was that made him so estimable. In fact, the more his reputation rose, the more contested his legacy became. By 2004, in the wake of the war in Iraq, American neo-conservatives and their "realist" critics were arguing over who was the legitimate heir of Reagan's policies.[43] On the left, certain liberals—un-able to deny Reagan's catalytic role in concluding the cold war—began to assert that Reagan had succeeded because he had given up his hard-line conservative ideology. It was Reagan's "pragmatism," they asserted, and his willingness to negotiate with the Soviets that had led him to "end" the cold war rather than "win" it.[44]

The most audacious of the liberal revisionists was the historian John Patrick Diggins in his *Ronald Reagan: Fate, Freedom, and the Making of History*. Diggins, who detested neoconservatives like Norman Podhoretz, set out to "rescue" Reagan from the "neocon hawks" and other "so-called Reaganites" who had allegedly taken the United States down a "trail of blunders" in the Middle East. In flat contravention of the Reagan victory school, Diggins claimed that Reagan had been a "reluctant cold warrior" whose greatness lay in turning himself from a hawk into a dove.[45]

Nor did Diggins stop there. In the sweep of modern history, he asserted, Reagan was not a conservative at all (at least by Burkean standards) but a freewheeling liberal in the tradition of Thomas Paine and Ralph Waldo Emerson. "Far from being a conservative," wrote Diggins, "Reagan was the great liberating spirit of modern American history, a political romantic impatient with the status quo."[46]

Diggins's controversial book—colored, as it was, in part, by current contentions—intrigued but failed to persuade most conservative reviewers.[47] His insistence, for instance, that Reagan was a radically "Emersonian optimist" who believed man to be innately good seemed to neglect the depth of Reagan's Christian upbringing and convictions, including his belief in prayer and his serene assurance that God had a purpose for his life.[48] But the liberal historian was correct to notice in Reagan a romantic, even utopian streak, which shocked and at times mortified his advisers. Nowhere was this trait more in evidence than in his increasingly bold pursuit of the abolition of nuclear weapons.[49]

"Dick, you know what I *really* want to be remembered for?" he said out of the blue to his pollster Richard Wirthlin one evening in 1983. "I want to be remembered as the president of the United States who brought a sense and reality of peace and security. I want to eliminate that awful fear that each of us feels sometimes when we get up in the morning knowing that the world could be destroyed through a nuclear holocaust." Astonished by this remark, Wirthlin became convinced that Reagan was "a man who was *obsessed* with peace."[50] On another occasion, during a conversation in 1986 with his hard-line arms control adviser, General Edward Rowny, Reagan blurted out, "I have a dream. I have a dream of a world without nuclear weapons. I want our children and grandchildren particularly to be free of these weapons."[51] And what is more, he pursued this vision all the way to the fateful summit conference with Gorbachev in Reykjavik. What was the engine driving Reagan's unwavering quest? In his 1990 autobiography, he gave his answer. He disclosed how he came to believe after the assassination attempt on him in 1981 that God had spared his life for a reason. His brush with death led him to believe that he had discerned this reason. The experience made him feel that "I should do whatever I could in the years God had given me to reduce the threat of nuclear war."[52]

Thus, just when it seemed that Reagan's triumphant march into the history books was secure and conservatives could say "mission accomplished," the spin-doctoring of his legacy took a most unusual turn. Until 2004 or so, conservatives had labored with increasing success to rescue Reagan from the sneering incomprehension of left-wing academics. Now a new battle for his legacy loomed, with liberals striving to claim at least a part of it for themselves.[53]

And so the question arose, as it had so often during Reagan's lifetime: "Who was that masked man?"[54] Had there, in fact, been *two* Reagans behind that good-humored facade? If so, how did the two of them fit together? And which, if either, was the dominant part of his innermost self? The "ideologue" or the "pragmatist"?[55] The crusader against Communism or the crusader against the bomb? The persistent cold warrior and scourge of the "evil empire" or the peace seeker who (in his own words) "placed a lot of faith in the simple power of human contact in solving problems"?[56]

One conclusion was certain: "the riddle of Reagan" had not yet been totally solved.[57] Historians of his life and presidency were not about to become unemployed. The argument about the man and his legacy had only begun.

REAGAN IN TIME

So how stands the legacy of Ronald Reagan in 2008? Historical interpretation is a never-ending process, subject to ideological crossfire and the vicissitudes of bunk-and-debunk. Still, it seems very likely that five achievements of Reagan will stand out in the fullness of time. First, at a moment of dangerous drift and national malaise, he restored his country's sense of self-confidence and its will to achieve greatness. Second, he bequeathed an ineffaceable example of optimism, grit, serenity, wit, and constructive use of the life he had been given to live. Reagan himself did not believe that his own personality was of much historical importance. He once remarked that he could understand why, two hundred years from now, people would be interested in his presidency, but not why they would be interested in *him*.[58] Here, perhaps, his modesty misled him. As with other notable American presidents, his personal qualities will continue to fascinate and inspire. He may not make it to Mount Rushmore, but he will long survive in the Mount Rushmore of our collective memory.

Third—and for this conservatives especially will always be indebted—he transmuted American conservatism from theory to practice, gave conservatives a successful presidency to defend (and a statesman to honor), and shifted the paradigm of political discourse for at least a generation. Fourth, he mobilized the resources—rhetorical, military, diplomatic, economic, and spiritual—that in one way or another put Communism and its Soviet empire on the road to extinction.

Finally, and perhaps most important, he gave us his words. With incandescent prose he revived America's sense of itself as a sweet land of liberty, selected by God for a great purpose. For so long as the United States of America survives as a free and independent polity, his vision of America's meaning will tug at our souls.

Of this legacy, historians will likely say, "Not bad, not bad at all."

Notes

1. In January 2008, when this essay was written, an Internet search for "presidential legacy" yielded 17,700 results, and an Internet search for "Bush legacy" produced 136,000 results.

2. George W. Bush, interview by Nadia Bilbassy-Charters, January 4, 2008, excerpt provided by the White House Office of Public Liaison.

3. George W. Bush, interview by Nahum Barnes and Shimon Shiffer, January 2, 2008, excerpt provided by the White House Office of Public Liaison.

4. Franklin Roosevelt established the first presidential library in 1941, and every succeeding president has done the same. In 1962 Roosevelt's immediate predecessor in office, Herbert Hoover, dedicated his own presidential library, which then became part of the system of presidential libraries administered by the National Archives.

5. Ronald Reagan, *An American Life* (New York: Simon and Schuster, 1990).

6. Ronald Reagan, farewell address to the nation (Washington, DC, January 11, 1989), Public Papers of President Ronald W. Reagan, Ronald Reagan Presidential Library, http://www.reagan.utexas.edu/archives/speeches/publicpapers.html (hereafter cited as Reagan Papers).

7. The project maintains a weblog, *Reagan's Legacy*, at http://reaganlegacy.blogspot.com/.

8. For more on this campaign, visit the Heritage Foundation's website, http://www.heritage.org/.

9. These figures are for Internet searches conducted in January 2008.

10. Feulner quoted in Rebecca Hagelin, "What Would Reagan Do?" *Townhall.com*, January 9, 2008, http://townhall.com/columnists/Rebecca Hagelin/2008/01/09/what_would_reagan_do.

11. Thomas W. Evans, *The Education of Ronald Reagan: The General Electric Years and the Untold Story of His Conversion to Conservatism* (New York: Columbia University Press, 2006), 195.

12. See Jeffrey Bell, "The Candidate and the Briefing Book," *Weekly Standard*, February 5, 2001, 21–26, esp. 26.

This point deserves emphasis. Long ago, Cardinal John Henry Newman asserted that Toryism is "loyalty to persons." In the case of modern American conservatives, one must respond, Not necessarily so. For them conservatism is loyalty to principle. Where putatively conservative politicians appear to deviate too far or too often from these beliefs, the politicians lose their following on the right. When, for example, Senator Barry Goldwater—a conservative hero in the 1960s—appeared to move toward the left (on social issues) in the 1970s and 1980s, his popularity among conservatives declined. As mentioned in the text below, the same thing happened (to a lesser extent) to President Reagan during his second term.

13. Paul Kengor, *God and Ronald Reagan: A Spiritual Life* (New York: Regan Books, 2004), 76–88.

14. See Evans, *Education of Ronald Reagan*, esp. 74–80; Lee Edwards, *The Essential Ronald Reagan: A Profile in Courage, Justice, and Wisdom* (Lanham, MD: Rowman and Littlefield, 2005), 54; and Reagan, *American Life*, 129.

15. Ronald Reagan, remarks at a reception honoring the *National Review* (Washington, DC, February 21, 1983), Reagan Papers.

16. Lou Cannon, *President Reagan: The Role of a Lifetime* (New York: Simon and Schuster, 1991), 180.

17. Ronald Reagan with Richard G. Hubler, *Where's the Rest of Me?* (New York: Duell, Sloan and Pearce, 1965), 297.

18. *Reagan: A Life in Letters*, ed. Kiron K. Skinner, Annelise Anderson, and Martin Anderson (New York: Free Press, 2003), 272.

19. Reagan quoted in Stephen F. Hayward, *The Age of Reagan: The Fall of the Old Liberal Order, 1964–1980* (Roseville, CA: Forum, 2001), 680.

20. Michael Kramer, "The Book Reagan Wants You to Read," *New York*, December 1, 1980, 23–24, 26.

21. William F. Buckley Jr., "Standing athwart History, Yelling Stop," *National Review*, November 19, 1955, republished in *National Review Online*, June 29, 2004, http://www.nationalreview.com/flashback/buckley200406290949.asp.

22. *Reagan: A Life in Letters*, 256, 257, 259; Thomas Paine, *Common Sense* (1776), quoted in ibid., 259.

23. Ronald Reagan, inaugural address (Washington, DC, January 20, 1981), Reagan Papers.

24. See, for example, Norman Podhoretz, "The Neo-conservative Anguish over Reagan's Foreign Policy," *New York Times Magazine*, May 2, 1982, 30–33, 88–89, 92, 96–97; Norman Podhoretz, "Appeasement by Any Other Name," *Commentary*, July 1983, 25–31; Patrick Glynn, "Reagan's Rush to Disarm," *Commentary*, March 1988, 19–28; Walter Laqueur, "Glasnost & Its Limits," *Commentary*, July 1988, 13–24; and John Ehrman, *The Rise of Neoconservatism: Intellectuals and Foreign Affairs, 1945–1994* (New Haven, CT: Yale University Press, 1995), 146–49, 174–76.

25. Margaret Thatcher, *The Downing Street Years* (New York: HarperCollins, 1993), 470–73. The British prime minister was greatly alarmed by how far Reagan and his colleagues "had been prepared to go." It seemed to her "as if there had been an earthquake beneath my feet." She soon flew to Washington DC and persuaded Reagan to issue a joint statement of clarification with which she was "well pleased."

26. Sheldon L. Richman, "The Sad Legacy of Ronald Reagan," *Free Market*, October 1988, http://mises.org/freemarket_detail.aspx?control=488.

27. For example, see "A Fond Farewell to the 'Gipper,'" *Human Events*, January 21, 1989, 1, 17.

28. Commager quoted in Charles Krauthammer, "Reluctant Cold Warriors," *Washington Post*, November 12, 1999, A35.

29. Slight variations of this aphorism are in circulation, all attributed to Reagan. The historian John Lewis Gaddis has shrewdly noted "Reagan's artful artlessness: his habit of *appearing* to know less than his critics did, of *seeming* to be adrift even as he proceeded quietly toward destinations he himself had chosen." John Lewis Gaddis, "Strategies of Containment: Post–Cold War Reconsiderations" (address at the Elliott School of International Affairs, George Washington University, Washington, DC, April 15, 2004), http://www.gwu.edu/~elliott/news/transcripts/gaddis.cfm.

30. Siena Research Institute, "FDR America's Greatest President," news release, August 19, 2002, http://lw.siena.edu/sri/results/2002/02AugPresidentsSurvey.htm.

31. Arthur Schlesinger Jr., "The Ultimate Approval Rating," *New York Times Magazine,* December 15, 1996, 46–51; Arthur Schlesinger Jr., "Rating the Presidents: Washington to Clinton," *Political Science Quarterly* 112 (Summer 1997): 179–90.

32. Alvin S. Felzenberg, "'There You Go Again': Liberal Historians and the *New York Times* Deny Ronald Reagan His Due," *Policy Review,* March–April 1997, 51–53; James Taranto and Leonard Leo, eds., *Presidential Leadership: Rating the Best and the Worst in the White House* (New York: Wall Street Journal Books, 2004). According to the scholars polled by Taranto and Leo, Reagan placed eighth among all the presidents, just behind Harry S. Truman and just ahead of Dwight D. Eisenhower.

33. Paul Kengor, "Reagan among the Professors," *Policy Review,* December 1999–January 2000, 15–27.

34. James MacGregor Burns, "Risks of the Middle," *Washington Post,* October 24, 1999, B7.

35. See Ronald Reagan, address at commencement exercises at the University of Notre Dame (Notre Dame, IN, May 17, 1981), Reagan Papers, and Ronald Reagan, remarks at the national convention of the National Association of Evangelicals (Orlando, FL, March 8, 1983), Reagan Papers.

36. See Marc Fisher, "The Old Warrior at the Wall," *Washington Post,* September 13, 1990, D1–D2, and Fred Barnes, "Covering the Gipper," *Weekly Standard,* February 5, 2001, 29.

37. See especially Peter Schweizer, *Reagan's War: The Epic Story of His Forty Year Struggle and Final Triumph over Communism* (New York: Doubleday, 2002), and Paul Kengor, *The Crusader: Ronald Reagan and the Fall of Communism* (New York: Regan Books, 2006).

38. Edmund Levin, "Reagan's Victory?" *Weekly Standard,* November 15, 2004, 31–34.

39. Gaddis, "Strategies of Containment."

40. *Reagan, in His Own Hand,* ed. Kiron K. Skinner, Annelise Anderson, and Martin Anderson (New York: Free Press, 2001).

41. Paul Lettow, *Ronald Reagan and His Quest to Abolish Nuclear Weapons* (New York: Random House, 2005), 243.

42. *The Reagan Diaries,* ed. Douglas Brinkley (New York: HarperCollins, 2007).

43. See, for example, Stefan Halper and Jonathan Clarke, "Would Ronald Reagan Have Attacked Iraq?" *American Spectator,* June 15, 2004, http://spectator.org/archives/2004/06/15/would-ronald-reagan-have-attac (originally published in the April 2004 issue of *American Spectator* as "Neoconservatism Is Not Reaganism"), and Peter J. Wallison, "Reagan, Iraq, and Neoconservatism," June 16, 2004, *American Spectator,* http://spectator.org/archives/2004/06/16/

reagan-iraq-and-neoconservatis. See also Jacob Heilbrunn, "A Uniter, not a Decider," *National Interest*, July–August 2007, 79–87.

44. John Patrick Diggins, "How Reagan Beat the Neocons," *New York Times*, June 11, 2004, A27.

45. John Patrick Diggins, *Ronald Reagan: Fate, Freedom, and the Making of History* (New York: Norton, 2007), xxi, xxii, 34; John Patrick Diggins, interview, *Washington Times*, February 7, 2007, A2.

46. Diggins, *Ronald Reagan*, xvii.

47. For respectful but critical assessments of Diggins's book by conservative scholars and journalists, see Rich Lowry, "The Liberal Reagan," *New York Times Book Review*, February 18, 2007, 21; Katherine Ernst, "Was Reagan a Liberal?" *City Journal*, March 2, 2007, http://www.city-journal.org/html/rev2007-03-02ke.html; Dan Seligman, "Warriors," *Commentary*, April 2007, 71–74; Peter J. Wallison, "Reagan Co-opted," *American Spectator*, July–August 2007, 68–75; and Steven F. Hayward, "Reagan and the Historians," *Claremont Review of Books* 7 (Fall 2007): 14–18. For Diggins's subsequent argument with Wallison, see "Whose Reagan? An Exchange," *American Spectator*, October 2007, 8–11.

48. Interestingly, the most systematic study of Reagan's religious faith—Paul Kengor's *God and Ronald Reagan*—contains not a single reference to Ralph Waldo Emerson.

49. On this point, see Lettow, *Reagan and His Quest*, 132–34, 234–35; Edward Rowny, interview by Stephen Knott, May 17, 2006, 14–16, Ronald Reagan Oral History Project, Presidential Oral History Program, Miller Center of Public Affairs, University of Virginia, http://millercenter.org/scripps/archive/oralhistories/reagan; and Kenneth L. Adelman, *The Great Universal Embrace: Arms Summitry—A Skeptic's Account* (New York: Simon and Schuster, 1989), 20, 67–70. Adelman, who served (by Reagan's appointment) as director of the U.S. Arms Control and Disarmament Agency from 1983 to 1987, described Reagan as an antinuclear "mystic" with a "visionary streak."

50. Richard B. Wirthlin with Wynton C. Hall, *The Greatest Communicator: What Ronald Reagan Taught Me about Politics, Leadership, and Life* (Hoboken, NJ: Wiley, 2004), 113–15. According to Wirthlin, this conversation occurred "just as his [Reagan's] economic policies were beginning to kick in and produce what would later become unprecedented economic growth." This would have been at the end of 1982 or (more likely) 1983.

51. Lettow, *Reagan and His Quest*, 196; Rowny, interview, 14.

52. Reagan, *American Life*, 269.

53. In his review of John Patrick Diggins's book, Rich Lowry remarked, "Across the political spectrum we are beginning to agree that Ronald Reagan was an important, even admirable, figure. What liberals and conservatives will probably never agree on is why." Lowry, "Liberal Reagan," 21.

54. This was the title of chapter 8 in Peggy Noonan's memoir, *What I Saw at the Revolution: A Political Life in the Reagan Era* (New York: Random House, 1990).

55. One of Reagan's most thorough biographers to date, Lou Cannon, has written that "on nearly all issues," Reagan "was simultaneously an ideologue and a pragmatist." Cannon, *President Reagan,* 185.

56. Reagan, *American Life,* 567.

57. Michael K. Deaver, *A Different Drummer: My Thirty Years with Ronald Reagan* (New York: HarperCollins, 2001), 2.

58. Reagan so expressed himself at a dinner of presidential biographers at which I was present in Washington DC on February 14, 1983.

MR. REAGAN GOES TO WASHINGTON

Stephen F. Knott

When Ronald Reagan took the oath of office on January 20, 1981, the new president had seen five of his immediate predecessors leave office under duress: Kennedy by assassination, Johnson forced into retirement by the Vietnam War, Nixon forced to resign, Ford defeated by Carter, Carter defeated by Reagan. Reagan's immediate predecessor, Jimmy Carter, appeared at times to be overwhelmed by the presidency, and despite, or perhaps because of, his renowned attention to detail, he never seemed to master the job. There was also a kind of cramped style to the Carter presidency, a sort of uninspired casualness that perhaps suited the nation's mood in the immediate aftermath of Watergate and Vietnam but did not wear well over time. All this changed with the arrival of the Reagans in Washington—the new president set the tone for his presidency by restoring all the trappings of presidential pomp and circumstance in his lavish inaugural ceremonies. In the proverbial tug-of-war that presidents seem to walk between Jeffersonian simplicity and high-toned Hamiltonianism, Ronald Reagan clearly leaned toward the latter in his proclivity for White House pageantry.

DOMESTIC POLICY: A FAST START

Reagan's presidency got off to a fast start, in part because of a transition that many political scientists and practitioners viewed as the model for an incoming presidency. Reagan also benefited from the fact that the revolutionary government of Iran decided to free the American hostages it had held for well over a year just minutes after the president was inaugurated. The new president focused on three goals for his first term: reducing income tax rates, balancing the federal budget, and increasing defense spending. In his inaugural address, Reagan claimed that the era of big government, ushered in by the New Deal and the Great Society, was over: "Government is not the solution to our problem; government is the problem." In the foreign affairs arena, Reagan struck a combative stance toward the Soviet Union; at his first press conference, the president accused the Soviet leadership of "reserv[ing] unto themselves the right to commit any crime, to lie, to cheat," and added that "the only morality they recognize is what will further their cause."[1] This opening rhetorical salvo against the Kremlin would be followed by more denunciations, culminating in Reagan's "evil empire" speech in March 1983.

Reagan's concerns about the Soviet Union had a significant impact on American domestic policy, particularly regarding the federal budget. Much to the despair of David Stockman, his whiz kid director of the Office of Management and Budget, Reagan decided to proceed with a program of tax rate cuts and large increases in defense spending, despite warnings that this could lead to a massive increase in the federal deficit. Stockman and Secretary of Defense Caspar Weinberger were locked in mortal combat in the early days of the administration, and each man viewed the other with suspicion. A number of Reagan's aides later recalled that the president would have liked to reduce the budget deficit but considered it the price he had to pay for his defense increases and his tax rate cuts. Reagan's tolerance of large deficits, which would become more pronounced as his presidency wore on, disturbed many of his supporters from his conservative base.

During his eight years in office, Ronald Reagan never once submitted a balanced budget to Congress, despite pledging during his 1980 campaign that this would be a priority of his presidency. The United States was $1.8 trillion deeper in the red by the time Reagan left the White House, and even the normally effervescent Gipper was forced to admit in his farewell address to the nation that his failure to balance the budget was his deepest disappointment. "I've been asked if I have any regrets. Well, I do. The deficit is one."[2]

Other elements of Reagan's fiscal and economic policy proved more popular and met with more success. The president gave top priority in 1981 to passage of his tax rate cuts, a defense increase, and domestic spending cuts. Although the latter ultimately went nowhere, the tax cuts and defense increases became policy after Reagan siphoned off the support of the so-called Boll Weevils, a group of mostly southern Democrats who deserted their party to support the president. Reagan's victories in Congress in 1981 were some of the most impressive legislative achievements since Lyndon Johnson's successes of 1964–1965. Through skillful use of direct appeals to the public and personal "massaging" of conservative Democrats, Reagan put together a bipartisan coalition in the Democrat-controlled House of Representatives that enacted key elements of his tax initiatives under the Economic Recovery Tax Act of 1981. Much of the credit was due to the skillful tactics of his legislative liaison, Max Friedersdorf, but also to Reagan's hard work. During the first weeks of 1981, Reagan held sixty-nine meetings with 467 members of the House and "worked the phones" as key votes approached.[3] He also developed an amiable relationship with his great adversary in the House of Representatives, Speaker Thomas P. "Tip" O'Neill. The bond that existed between O'Neill and Reagan deepened in the aftermath of the assassination attempt on the president. But it was not always sweetness and light between the Speaker and the president; O'Neill was furious that Reagan was able to lure forty votes from Democratic members of the House to pass his tax package. By the end of 1981, the American economy was seen, rightly or wrongly, to be Reagan's economy. "Reaganomics" was the catchall term applied to his economic program, and as Friedersdorf noted, from that point on, Reagan would be "blamed if anything goes wrong . . . snow, bubonic plague."[4]

Within days of the passage of his tax rate cuts, Reagan was confronted with a strike by the nation's air traffic controllers that threatened to drag an already lethargic economy deeper into recession. The Professional Air Traffic Controllers Organization (PATCO) went on strike on August 3, 1981, demanding increased compensation and reduced overtime requirements. In an announcement made in the White House Rose Garden, Reagan warned the controllers that if they did not return to their jobs within forty-five hours, they would be fired. For many observers, this signaled an assertion of presidential muscle that had not been seen since President Kennedy's confrontation with the steel industry in 1962. PATCO had been one of the few unions that endorsed Ronald Reagan for president in 1980, so Reagan's hard-line stance against the controllers caught many Americans by surprise.

Foreign Policy: Overcoming Criticism

Whereas Reagan's domestic initiatives met with some success during his first year in office, in the foreign policy arena he was accused of aggravating cold war tensions by bluntly criticizing the Soviet Union and by engaging in the biggest defense buildup in the history of the world. Halfway into Reagan's first term, many reputable observers were convinced that the cold war was on the verge of turning hot. Throughout his first term, Ronald Reagan's reputation for "Truman-like" plain speaking toward the Soviet Union was the subject of considerable controversy. His hard-line rhetoric contributed to the rise of antinuclear protests on the part of groups advocating a nuclear freeze, a movement that attempted to convince both of the superpowers to freeze their nuclear stockpiles as an initial step toward disarmament. At his first press conference as president, Reagan shocked many observers with his blunt assessment of the character of the Soviet leadership, noting that the geriatrics in the Kremlin reserved the right to commit "any crime, to lie, to cheat" to advance their interests.[5] In one area, however, Reagan disappointed many of his hawkish advisers by following through in 1981 on a campaign pledge to lift the grain embargo enacted by President Carter following the Soviet invasion of Afghanistan.

The following year, in an address to the British Parliament, Reagan escalated his anti-Soviet rhetoric, asking his audience, "What, then, is our course? Must civilization perish in a hail of fiery atoms? Must freedom wither in a quiet, deadening accommodation with totalitarian evil?" Answering his own question with a line borrowed from Leon Trotsky, Reagan proclaimed that "the march of freedom and democracy . . . will leave Marxism-Leninism on the ash heap of history."[6] In March 1983, Reagan ratcheted up the rhetorical ante in a speech delivered to the National Association of Evangelicals in Orlando, Florida. The so-called evil empire speech, widely derided at the time, was perhaps the most notable speech of Reagan's presidency. The phrase "evil empire" made it into the final text in part because of the assumption that the speech to the evangelical group would receive little media attention, but, perhaps more important, Reagan was determined that it remain in the text. The president put his own stamp on the speech in a number of important ways, including altering the most memorable line in the draft: "Now and forever, the Soviet Empire is an evil empire." The president deleted the first three words of that sentence, for he believed that the Soviet Union was not long for this world.[7] He made another critical change to the text: an early draft read, "Surely historians will see there the focus of evil in the modern world"; Reagan changed it to read, "They are the focus of evil in the modern world."[8]

The "evil empire" speech reinforced Reagan's image as a gunslinging cowboy, particularly in a jittery Western Europe that would receive its first shipment of U.S. Pershing II and ground-launched cruise missiles that fall. These missiles were designed to counter the Soviet Union's intermediate-range missile, the SS-20, which had been deployed throughout Eastern Europe and parts of Asia in the late 1970s. Even some of Reagan's most devoted admirers thought the president had gone too far. In the midst of the tense autumn of 1983, the Soviets aggravated East-West tensions by shooting down a Korean Airlines 747 passenger jet with 269 passengers onboard, including a member of Congress and 60 other Americans. Reagan was outraged, but he rejected suggestions from his more hawkish advisers for "drastic responses," as Secretary of State George Shultz put it, to the Soviet action.[9]

The cold war struggle between the United States and the Soviet Union was at the top of Reagan's agenda throughout his presidency. He was elected president primarily on a promise to repair the American economy, but Communism and the threat of nuclear war were his chief concerns. In regard to foreign and security policy, especially with respect to the cold war, I am convinced the American people did not realize they were electing a radical, an idealist, a dreamer. Reagan's fear of nuclear war was little understood at the time, particularly among his critics in the nuclear freeze movement, but also by some prominent members of his own administration. He viewed the doctrine of mutually assured destruction, which held American and Soviet civilians as hostages to preserve the peace, as immoral. His objections to both Communism and nuclear weapons were rooted in his strong religious beliefs, and the depths of those beliefs were not understood by many of his contemporaries.

Although the Soviet newspaper *Pravda* was not known for its fidelity to the truth, its assessment of President Reagan as a character out of a work of Mark Twain, a midwestern innocent in the White House, was dead-on. As presidents, Jimmy Carter and Ronald Reagan were closer than we might think; both were as far removed from the cold, calculating, at times cynical presidencies of Lyndon Johnson and Richard Nixon as one can get. Reagan repeatedly shocked his hawkish advisers with such radical schemes as proposing to share Strategic Defense Initiative (SDI) technology with the Soviets and to eliminate nuclear weapons from the superpower arsenals. (One of Reagan's favorite anecdotes, which he shared with Gorbachev and his own national security advisers and which they later dubbed his "little green men" obsession, was to raise the specter of an attack on earth by aliens and point out how important it would be for all nations and all human beings to band together.) As Kenneth Adelman, former director of the Arms Control and Disarmament Agency, later observed,

> Until I got in the arms control business in a serious way, I did not realize how antinuclear Ronald Reagan was. I thought he supported the MX, he supported all our nuclear build-up on that, the B-1 bomber, and everything else that we had going. The fact was he couldn't stand nuclear weapons; he wanted to get rid of nuclear weapons. So as much as the antinuclear wave was going around, Ronald Reagan would have been right in the movement. He thought the way to do it was SDI. But Reagan was just very antinuclear. Like *The Day After* [an antinuclear film that aired on American television], it would exactly represent Reagan's view. I'd never met an antinuclear hawk before in my life. It was just part of Reagan's make-up.[10]

Reagan's national security adviser, Frank Carlucci, noted that Reagan viewed the accident at Chernobyl as the opening event in the fulfillment of the biblical prophecy of Armageddon, and noted the president's heartfelt desire to eliminate nuclear weapons. "People accuse him of being against arms control, but he was the biggest arms control advocate you've seen."[11]

Reagan's disdain for the doctrine of mutually assured destruction and his innate optimism in America's technological prowess led him to embrace the concept of missile defense and propose his SDI. In a televised address delivered in March 1983, a little over two weeks after the "evil empire" speech, Reagan outlined his "vision of the future which offers hope." He called for the nation to "embark on a program to counter the awesome Soviet missile threat with measures that are defensive." He added, "What if free people could live secure in the knowledge that their security did not rest upon the threat of instant U.S. retaliation to deter a Soviet attack, that we could intercept and destroy strategic ballistic missiles before they reached our own soil or that of our allies?"[12] Reagan's SDI proposal, tacked on at the end of a speech devoted to the defense budget, took many around the world by surprise and even caught a number of his own national security and foreign policy team members off guard. SDI was attacked from the start as a fantasy, and an expensive fantasy at that. Many scientists were skeptical that an effective system could be created that would protect the United States (and its allies) from ballistic missiles. It was also argued that even if such a shield could be developed, there were alternative, "lower-tech" methods of evading missiles. SDI was quickly labeled a boondoggle and given a more familiar name by Senator Edward Kennedy of Massachusetts: "star wars," a brand that stuck.

The notion that Reagan had a master plan to bankrupt the Soviet Union, through SDI and other initiatives, is a subject of controversy to this day. There is a difference of opinion on this even among veterans of his administration, with some of his more hawkish advisers contending that he had such an agenda and others, particularly George Shultz, dismissing it as nonsense. To the end of his life, Caspar Weinberger believed that the key elements of Reagan's campaign to bring down the Soviet Union were SDI, rhetorical attacks, conventional defense buildup, and covert operations against the Soviet Union and its proxies, along with a "change in determination."[13]

Weinberger's hard-line approach toward the Soviet Union was reflected in the president's so-called zero-option proposal, in which Reagan called for the removal of all of the Soviet SS-20 intermediate-range missiles from Europe and Asia, in return for the United States' canceling its deployment of Pershing II and ground-launched cruise missiles in Western Europe. When Reagan announced this proposal in November 1981, it was deemed "nonnegotiable" by many in the media and by many Western arms control experts, and dismissed by the Kremlin. Nevertheless, certain elements of the zero option were later included in the Intermediate-Range Nuclear Forces (INF) Treaty signed at the White House in December 1987 by President Reagan and Mikhail Gorbachev. But during the first years of the Reagan presidency, the potential for such a sweeping arms reduction would have struck many as pure fantasy. The extent to which Reagan had a strategy to make this happen is subject to dispute, as is the question of how much of a difference his SDI program and his anti-Soviet rhetoric had on the collapse of the Soviet regime.

What is indisputable is that Ronald Reagan and his "friend" Mikhail Gorbachev radically changed the face of world politics. Ten months after Reagan left office, the Berlin Wall fell, and in December 1991, the Soviet Union ceased to exist. After the INF Treaty breakthrough, there had been a profound relaxation in relations between the two superpowers, typified by Reagan's visit to Moscow in May 1988, when he strolled through Red Square with the Soviet leader and found time to kiss a few babies along the way. In a remarkably short period of time, the two leaders had managed to transform superpower relations to the point where some began to talk about a new world order based on peace and prosperity.

One of the most memorable events from Reagan's visit to Moscow was his speech to the students at Moscow State University, where the old cold warrior extolled the virtues of capitalism and celebrated the creative dynamism of free societies. Whether the credit for the dramatic transformation of superpower relations belongs to Reagan or Gorbachev remains a subject of dispute, but Reagan's high-stakes diplomacy surprised his most vocal detractors on the right and the left. Some members of Reagan's own team were taken aback at how well he performed. In his four encounters with Gorbachev, Reagan showed little interest in the details of arms control, but he was animated in his defense of religious and political dissidents inside the USSR.

Margaret Thatcher would later credit President Reagan for winning the cold war without firing a shot. Thatcher aside, the extent to which Reagan deserves credit for ending the superpower conflict remains a contested issue among historians and political scientists, although not surprisingly most of his former advisers and confidants are convinced their man deserves the accolades. The president's supporters argue that Reagan's defense buildup and SDI led the Soviets to seek an accord, while others tend to give the bulk of the credit to Gorbachev's willingness to break with the practices of his predecessors. Ronald Reagan's strengths as a leader came from his oft-noted communication skills but also from lesser-known skills, such as his talents as a negotiator and a cheerleader, his abilities to set clear policy goals and to delegate, and his persistence.

Executive Weaknesses

President Reagan had some glaring weaknesses as a chief executive, and while his ability to delegate responsibility and allow subordinates to bask in the success of his administration was a source of strength, it was also a source of weakness, as the Iran-contra scandal demonstrated. Reagan was notoriously fond of delegating, and for much of his presidency his hands-off style worked well. But that system required a strong hand, or set of hands, to supervise the underlings. For most of Reagan's first term, his troika of Chief of Staff James Baker, Deputy Chief of Staff Michael Deaver, and White House Counselor Edwin Meese had balanced each other quite well. Despite their differences, they kept the administration on message and provided coherent guidance to those down the chain of command. In 1985, a new White House chief of staff, Donald Regan, had decided to let the National Security Council function more or less on its own, even though he liked to boast that he was the "prime minister" of the Reagan court. This dysfunctional arrangement led to the disastrous Iran-contra affair, the worst crisis of Reagan's presidency, one that could have led to his impeachment. In the end, the president avoided impeachment and managed to leave office in 1989 a relatively popular president. But in the interim, jokes about his detached management style became routine, and his tough talk against terrorism rang hollow. Throughout the scandal, Reagan was disturbed by the fact that many Americans no longer took him at his word, and some of those close to him observed that his sunny outlook on life seemed, for a time, to have disappeared.

Another problem that dogged Reagan throughout his two terms in office was the constant infighting that occurred among various factions in the White House, each of whom felt it had the president's best interests at heart. Leaking became a high art during the Reagan years, and these leaks were often designed to undermine the standing of some member of Reagan's inner circle. The constant flood of leaks contributed to the perception of a president who did not have control of his own White House. Reagan hated dealing with personnel matters, and his wife often handled them. As longtime Reagan campaign guru Stuart Spencer observed, "No one else will say this, but I say this: she was the personnel director. She didn't have anything to do with policy. She'd say something every now and then and he'd look at her and say, 'Hey,

Mommy, that's my role.' She'd shut up. But when it came to who is the Chief of Staff, who is the political director, who is the press secretary, she had input because he didn't like personnel decisions."[14]

These quarrels were frequently reported in the press as struggles between the pragmatists (James Baker, Michael Deaver [who often acted at Mrs. Reagan's behest], and Richard Darman) and the true believers, or Reaganauts (Ed Meese, William Clark, Richard Allen, Lyn Nofziger). For much of the president's first term, there was persistent sniping from the right directed at Reagan's somewhat surprising choice of chief of staff, James Baker, a man with deep ties to George H. W. Bush and Gerald Ford but no connection with Ronald Reagan. For some of the true believers, particularly Nofziger, the selection of Baker prevented Reagan, a "great" president, from becoming "greater." During the first term, there were a number of leaks to the press dealing with the working arrangement within the so-called troika, with Baker serving as chief of staff, Deaver as deputy chief of staff, and Meese as counselor to the president. Meese was the target of a number of stories in the media suggesting that he was in over his head and that he lacked basic management skills. Many of the true believers were convinced that these leaks could be traced to Baker.[15]

Civil Rights Oversights

I would add to the list of criticisms of Reagan's presidency his tin ear on civil rights. How different would American politics be if Reagan had genuinely reached out to African Americans? In crude political terms, perhaps 15–20 percent of African Americans would now view themselves as Republicans instead of the single digits the GOP routinely polls among African Americans. Reagan's gratuitous remarks regarding Dr. Martin Luther King Jr. and his suggestion that King may have been a Communist did little to improve race relations in the United States and certainly tarnished Reagan's reputation as a man of civility. President Reagan abdicated his leadership when it came to civil rights; he did not use his vaunted communication skills to attempt to bridge the gap, to keep the dialogue alive, that he first suggested to the National Association for the Advancement of Colored People in the summer of 1981. Reagan acknowledged his failure in this area, noting in his published collection of speeches, "For all of my so-called powers of communication, I was never able to convince many black citizens of my commitment to their needs. They often mistook my belief in keeping the government out [of] the average American's life as a cover for doing nothing about racial injustice."[16]

The issues of the Reagan years, still very much with us today, were frequently couched in polarized language from the right and the left, making any genuine compromise almost impossible. But true presidential leadership would have entailed rising above the hurt that Reagan said he felt from being accused of being a racist and reaching out with some conciliatory gestures. The establishment of the King holiday, which should have been such an occasion, was instead compromised by Reagan's implication that King was a Communist sympathizer.

Reagan demonstrated on other occasions a capacity for obtuseness concerning racial matters, for example, by opening his 1980 campaign in the county where three civil rights workers were murdered in 1964. He did not mention the murders and instead made a plea for states' rights, which did not help his reputation. His 1980 platform was notable for its absence of nonbinding lip service he could have paid painlessly to the notion of equal rights under the law. In his first term, Reagan stopped meeting with the Congressional Black Caucus, which contributed further to an image of indifference. Granted, the caucus was dominated by left-wing critics, but for a president who said on numerous occasions that he hoped for a dialogue, it was a strange strategy. One wishes the president had paid more attention to conservatives such as Jack Kemp, whose vision of an "opportunity society," including enterprise zones and tenant ownership of public housing, only briefly captured the Republican imagination. It seemed at times that Ronald Reagan truly believed that America's race problem had been solved. In light of this, he seems to have accepted Patrick Moynihan's earlier advice to Richard Nixon and adopted a policy of "benign neglect" on racial matters. No serious attempt was made to lure black voters away from the Democratic Party, despite the occasional dreams of such realignment by Reagan-era Republican strategists.

IMAGE MANAGEMENT

There was also an element of Hollywood superficiality in certain aspects of Reagan's presidency. The late Michael Deaver was the guardian and projector of the president's image, which was certainly as calculated as the images that came out of the Kennedy White House. For instance, Lyn Nofziger and William Casey didn't look quite right for certain roles, while James Baker did, and as a consequence Casey and Nofziger were denied more public roles for which they were eminently qualified.[17] One could also note other elements of California superficiality and wackiness woven into the fabric of the Reagan years, including Nancy Reagan's reliance on astrology and Reagan's friendship with the psychic Jeane Dixon.

CHARACTER AND PHILOSOPHY

Nonetheless, Ronald Reagan was a prince of a man, and like his hero Franklin Roosevelt, he had a first-class temperament. While toughness and resolve were parts of his character, it was Reagan's gentle nature and his repeated acts of kindness that his inner circle most vividly recalls. He was a man of civility, who could reach out to Speaker Tip O'Neill even after O'Neill characterized Reagan's wife as Marie Antoinette in a Bill Blass dress. He was generous to other partisan critics of his, including Edward Kennedy and his family. And it goes without saying that Ronald Reagan loved the American military.

I will leave it to others to interpret the nuances of Reagan's political philosophy, but at his core he was a descendant of the antifederalist, Jeffersonian streak in American politics. He believed in universal human rights, and his favorite quote was from Thomas Paine, to the effect that we have it in our power to make the world over again. For Reagan, government was the problem; it was *the* obstacle that prevented Americans from pursuing happiness. Yet this antifederalist admirer of states' rights and advocate of strict judicial interpretation immersed himself in Hamiltonian trappings and followed a strain of Hamiltonian power politics in his approach to international relations.

Reagan was often described as our most ideological president, yet he was in fact one of our most issue-oriented presidents. This will come as a shock to those who cling to the notion of a simpleminded, 3 × 5 card–reading president who followed the directives of his staff and was incapable of distinguishing fact from movie fiction. Ironically, Reagan was not particularly interested in politics; in fact, there was a shyness about him that led him to disdain some of the backslapping rituals of the vocation. As Stuart Spencer observed,

Ronald Reagan is a shy person. People don't understand this.
. . . The first time in '65, we took him to West Covina. I remember the town. I took him out to West Covina to somebody's house for a fundraiser. They probably had fifty to seventy-five people there. He walked in with Nancy. Or he came with me, I can't remember now. He goes over to the corner of a room and stands there. These people are milling around here and the bar is over here. I'm watching all this. Finally I walked over to him and I said, "Ron, you've got to get out and mix. You've got to rub shoulders." He was used to people coming to him. I said, "You've got to go press the hands. You've got to move it." He didn't like doing that. He didn't like doing that. Not that he was above all that. He was a shy person and he didn't want to walk up to you and say, "I'm Ronald Reagan and I'm running for Governor." Now, the exact opposite to that was Nelson Rockefeller. He'd work a room if there were three people in it. It was always, "Hi ya, fella. Hi ya, fella." Just the opposite type of person. Reagan slowly developed a tolerance for working a room and doing those things. That's the best way I can describe it. At communication, one-on-one, he was not very good. At global, big communication, the stage, he was fabulous.[18]

Reagan went into politics for the purest and the noblest of reasons: he believed he could make a difference, especially in regard to Communism abroad and "big government" at home. He was the personification in our time of the classical republican conception of citizenship: the yeoman who leaves his plow, or in this case his camera, and spends part of his life in the public arena, all the while remaining skeptical of the very government he is called to serve. Reagan was an antifederalist to the core, which in post–Civil War, post–New Deal America was, and remains, a hard sell. Reagan's hostility to "big government" led to certain failings in his presidency, including an utter lack of interest, at times disregard, for certain domestic policies and agencies that he considered destructive to the character of a free people. This was most apparent in his indifference, for a time, to the growing AIDS crisis and in his neglect of agencies such as the Department of Housing and Urban Development, which provided a haven for a number of corrupt individuals.

Ronald Reagan on Balance

The Ronald Reagan I came to partially understand through my chairmanship of the Ronald Reagan Oral History Project, which conducted interviews of forty-seven of his longtime associates, was repulsed by cynicism—he saw the best in people and rejected the politics of personal destruction. He had little affection for the federal government he presided over, yet he never viewed his opponents as any less patriotic or public-spirited than he. Reagan was the personification of civility, was utterly without guile, and possessed an unbridled optimism that was quintessentially American. It is somewhat astounding that this remarkably genial person, the anti-Nixon if you will, who presided over a White House that was frequently described as a fun place to work, made it to the top of the American system. That this man became president is a reminder to all of us in these cynical, hyperpartisan times that there is an alternative to the vision of American politics as blood sport, that in fact it is even possible, as Reagan might say if he were here today, that there are leaders who are genuinely public-spirited and devoted to the common good.

Ronald Reagan was a good and decent man, a near-great president, but not a great president. As much as it pains me to say this, his age, his stamina, and his inherent inability to control the White House personnel situation damaged his effectiveness as a president. Reagan's presidency was characterized by a torrent of leaks, by frequent staff infighting and backbiting, and by a failed domestic agenda. Judging him by the standards he set, his major domestic goals of balancing the budget and dismantling the welfare or "nanny" state failed. Perhaps Ronald Reagan would have had a more successful presidency if he had gotten angry more often. It is almost as if he did not have the stomach for that fight; he was not as tough as his friend Margaret Thatcher. As the British popular historian Paul Johnson has observed, "While Reagan charmed and mesmerized, she had to bludgeon."[19] Having said this, I acknowledge that domestic concerns were always secondary to Reagan's desire to end the cold war or, should I say, win the cold war. That of course was a remarkable triumph, and one that earns him the status of a near-great president.

Oddly, one of our most media-friendly presidents remains to this day one of the most elusive in terms of capturing what made him tick.

If you want to get a sense of the interior Reagan, and here I am going to commit heresy, read Edmund Morris's *Dutch*. I think over time the book will grow in stature, and despite its destructive device of inserting a fictional character into a work of nonfiction, and despite also its ignoring many of the major political events of Reagan's presidency, it is as fine a portrait of Reagan as you will get. There was almost unanimous condemnation of *Dutch* from Reagan insiders, although Reagan's daughter Patti Davis wrote that Morris showed her "the father I never knew." She added, "I still don't fully understand my father. After all those years of exhaustive research, even Edmund says the man is a mystery. But because of Edmund's book, I have more clues, more threads to tie together. . . . But there are people who can never really be known, who will always be partly in shadow, and I was born to such a man."[20]

It is impossible to find one excerpt from the Ronald Reagan Oral History Project that captures Ronald Reagan the man and the president, but the following anecdote helps us partially understand him. Kenneth Adelman said,

> I remember one time in the Oval Office he was looking out and there was a bunch of people chopping things and the forest rangers standing out on the South Lawn, and [William] Clark says, "Mr. President, Ken's here to take you to the Situation Room" or something. We were getting ready for the next round or summit or whatever it was. Reagan keeps looking out and this sound gets louder and he says, "I hear you, Bill. Just wish I was doing what those fellows are doing instead of going to all these stupid meetings hours at a time."
>
> I thought to myself, in the history of the United States, 200 years, we've had forest rangers who imagined themselves as President, but I can't imagine a President imagining himself as a forest ranger before. Here he was, dying to be a forest ranger.[21]

One must avoid the temptation to canonize Ronald Reagan. He had his flaws; for instance, he frequently misspoke at press conferences and was indifferent to personnel issues, and in certain domestic policy arenas he left the nation worse than he found it. But it is hard, after participating in all forty-seven oral history interviews, not to feel a certain affection for this man. What Reagan once observed of John F. Kennedy could easily apply to him: "Everything we saw him do seemed to portray a huge enjoyment of life. He seemed to grasp from the beginning that life is one fast-moving train, and you have to jump aboard and hold on to your hat and relish the sweep of the wind as it rushes by. You have to enjoy the journey; it's unthankful not to. . . . [I] think that's how his country remembers him, in his joy."[22]

High-Water Marks

Ronald Reagan's communication skills set a high standard for his successors to follow, for he elevated the presidential bully pulpit to a level of excellence not heard since the days of John F. Kennedy. His sunny optimism helped restore the people's faith in their nation and in the American presidency. Gone was the talk from the Carter years of a crippled presidency and the need to revamp the Constitution and import a parliamentary system to replace our system of checks and balances. Ronald Reagan's words will remain with us long after his policies are forgotten: for instance, his memorable "evil empire" speech and his appeal to Mikhail Gorbachev to "tear down this wall." His pledge to leave Marxism and Leninism on "the ash heap of history" likely contributed to the end of the Soviet Union by inspiring dissidents behind the iron curtain. His rhetoric during periods of national mourning buoyed the nation time and again: during the *Challenger* disaster of 1986 and during the memorial service for the American soldiers killed during a Christmastime plane crash in Newfoundland in 1985. His comments on Anne Frank at the Bergen-Belsen concentration camp, his remarks at the fortieth anniversary of D-day at Pointe du Hoc, France, and his tribute to the Unknown Soldier from the Vietnam conflict at Arlington National Cemetery in 1984 were some of the most moving rhetoric regarding war and heroism in the history of the American presidency. In the end, Reagan's words, like those of Thomas Jefferson, Abraham Lincoln, and Franklin Roosevelt, may prove to be his most durable legacy.

Notes

1. Reagan quoted in Stephen Knott and Jeffrey L. Chidester, *The Reagan Years* (New York: Facts on File, 2005), 343, 348–49.

2. *Public Papers of the Presidents of the United States: Ronald Reagan, 1988–89* (Washington, DC: GPO), 2:1721.

3. Knott and Chidester, *Reagan Years,* 39.

4. Friedersdorf quoted in ibid., 41.

5. Reagan quoted in ibid., 66.

6. Ronald Reagan, *Speaking My Mind* (New York: Simon and Schuster, 1989), 112, 118.

7. John Patrick Diggins, *Ronald Reagan: Fate, Freedom, and the Making of History* (New York: Norton, 2007), 29.

8. Paul Kengor, *God and Ronald Reagan: A Spiritual Life* (New York: Regan Books, 2004), 247.

9. George P. Shultz, *Turmoil and Triumph: My Years as Secretary of State* (New York: Scribner, 1993), 364.

10. Kenneth Adelman, interview by Jeff Chidester, Stephen Knott, and Robert Strong, September 30, 2003, 38, Ronald Reagan Oral History Project, Presidential Oral History Program, Miller Center of Public Affairs, University of Virginia, http://millercenter.org/scripps/archive/oralhistories/reagan (hereafter cited as Reagan Oral History Project).

11. Frank Carlucci, interview by Stephen Knott, Philip Zelikow, and Don Oberdorfer, August 28, 2001, 42, Reagan Oral History Project.

12. Reagan quoted in Knott and Chidester, *Reagan Years,* 404.

13. Caspar Weinberger, interview by Stephen Knott and Russell L. Riley, November 19, 2002, 31, Reagan Oral History Project.

14. Stuart Spencer, interview by Paul B. Freedman, Stephen Knott, Russell L. Riley, and James Sterling Young, November 15–16, 2001, 12, Reagan Oral History Project.

15. Lyn Nofziger, interview by Stephen Knott and Russell L. Riley, March 6, 2003, 39–40, Reagan Oral History Project.

16. Ronald Reagan, *Speaking My Mind: Selected Speeches* (New York: Simon and Schuster, 1989), 163.

17. See, for instance, Nofziger, interview, 41, in which he comments on the selection of James Baker as chief of staff: "Nancy likes stylish people, and Baker certainly is, on the surface, a class act. The other people they brought in, they're Ivy Leaguers and that kind of thing, and I think Nancy was impressed by him."

18. Spencer, interview, 26–27.

19. Paul Johnson, "Heroes: What Great Statesmen Have to Teach Us," *Imprimis,* December 2007, 7.

20. Patti Davis, "Finally Seeing My Father—through Edmund's Eyes," *Washington Post,* October 10, 1999, B1.

21. Adelman, interview, 50.

22. Ronald Reagan, remarks at a fund-raising reception for the John F.

Kennedy Library Foundation (McLean, VA, June 24, 1985), Public Papers of President Ronald W. Reagan, Ronald Reagan Presidential Library, http://www .reagan.utexas.edu/archives/speeches/publicpapers.html.

Reagan's Legacy, Bush's Burden

Paul G. Kengor

What is the legacy of Ronald Reagan? It is multifaceted, from the forging of a powerful Republican coalition that transformed the Electoral College for a generation, to the remaking of the political composition of the South, to the shift from a government favoring wealth redistribution to one that champions the market, to the sudden and genuine rebirth in American morale and patriotism that was felt immediately as the nation left the malaise of the 1970s and headed toward the shining city of the 1980s.

Most notably, the Reagan legacy was most deeply felt in foreign policy, in those footprints in the sand the fortieth president left across history and the world stage. And it is that legacy that, ironically, became a burden for President George W. Bush as he, too, sought to leave his impact on the annals of world history. And it will remain a burden for other presidents in the near future as well.

Legacy of Success

Before getting to that comparison between the fortieth and forty-third presidents, we need to carefully consider that Reagan legacy of success in foreign policy, specifically the cold war—the greatest, longest-enduring political and ideological conflict of the last century. Reagan contributed mightily to the end of that conflict and the end of the Soviet empire. It is utterly essential that we understand the near consensus on that point among so many of those who labor in this prickly scholarly vineyard that seems to spurn consensus.

The fact is that Ronald Reagan, because of that cold war achievement, is now consistently rated among the most successful presidents in all of American history—even by liberals, who, as all surveys attest, compose the vast majority of academia and media.

A long list of the most prestigious presidential scholars—most of whom in their wildest dreams would never have voted for Reagan—today rank Reagan quite favorably: Thomas Mann, Sidney Milkis, John W. Sloan, David Mervin, Stephen Skowronek, James T. Patterson, Robert Dallek, Matthew Dallek, and Alonzo Hamby, to cite a few.[1] George Mason University's Hugh Heclo maintains that Reagan was a "man of ideas" in the estimable company of Jackson, Madison, and Jefferson.[2] There are similar appraisals from giants like Harvard's dean of presidential scholars, the late Richard Neustadt, from popular historian and Pulitzer Prize winner David McCullough, from bestselling presidential historian Michael Beschloss, and from the likes of Yale's John Lewis Gaddis, the leading cold war historian.[3] James MacGregor Burns, the FDR scholar, says Reagan will be remembered as a "great" or at least "near-great" president.[4]

Reagan is even faring well in certain surveys of academics, nearly all of whom are politically liberal. This is not a skewed verdict, prompted, say, by surveys done in the immediate weeks following Reagan's passing in June 2004, when sympathies were high. For example, consider C-SPAN's 2000 survey of American presidents, in which Reagan was rated the eleventh-best president ever, which is an excellent rating—one that would rate Reagan a "high-average" or "near-great" president. At best, Reaganites in 2000 had hoped that their guy would make it into the "average" category in these surveys.[5]

The C-SPAN panel ranked the presidents in ten categories. In some of these, Reagan rated quite impressively. For instance, remarkably, he ranked fourth best among all chief executives—ever—in the category of "public persuasion," behind only FDR, Teddy Roosevelt, and Lincoln and ahead of JFK, Washington, Jackson, Jefferson, Wilson, and other chief executives renowned for their rhetoric.

Importantly, Reagan's strong showing in the survey was hardly the result of a stacked deck. C-SPAN's panel comprised fifty-eight well-known scholars, primarily academics, nearly all liberal. The list included top names like Douglas Brinkley, Andrew Burstein, Robert Dallek, Joseph Ellis, Robert Ferrell, Alonzo Hamby, Melvin Small, and Sheldon Stern. Evidence of their liberal Democrat credentials is seen in the survey. They rated FDR second greatest overall, Woodrow Wilson sixth,

JFK eighth—a vast exaggeration that simply cannot be defended—and LBJ tenth.

More, the only Reagan biographers in the C-SPAN bunch were *Washington Post* journalists Lou Cannon and Haynes Johnson, neither of which is anywhere near the right end of the spectrum. Johnson wrote perhaps the most demeaning contemporary account of Reagan, *Sleepwalking through History.* Another participant was the late Stephen Ambrose, who went out of his way to trash Reagan—completely out of context—in the epilogue of his revised edition of his biography of Richard Nixon.

In essence, then, in this 2000 C-SPAN survey, here is what happened: a group of left-wing scholars, surely not Reagan supporters while he was in office, and not converts to conservatism, decided that this most conservative of presidents was one of the best presidents. This was quite a testimony. True success comes when your contemporary opponents step back only a decade later, reevaluate, and do a 180-degree turn, deeming you a success. This survey was another win for the Gipper.

Another poll was done in 2000 by a group of academics selected by the *Wall Street Journal* and the Federalist Society. While the *Wall Street Journal* is an editorially conservative newspaper, the news section is not conservative. More, the list of academics surveyed was not a conservative group. A total of seventy-eight historians, political scientists, and even legal scholars were surveyed. Reagan placed as the eighth-best president in history in this poll, putting him in the "near-great" category. The group also rated him history's single most underrated president.[6]

This was one survey that made a strong goodwill effort at attempted ideological balance, to the extent that can be done in academe. Indeed, any sample of academe is going to be tilted to the left simply because of the overwhelming number of liberals who teach at colleges. Most of these presidential surveys are merely affirmations of the political bias of academics in the social sciences and humanities.

Thus, in both these surveys, it is all the more remarkable that Reagan ranked as well as he did, especially only a decade removed from his presidency. To be sure, one can find academic surveys where Reagan does not rate as well, but that is to be expected from a group of academics who self-identify in surveys as more than 90 percent liberal and spent the 1980s teaching their students that Reagan slept through cabinet meetings.

Significantly, this is only an examination of academia. Journalism follows the same pattern, and that is especially the case for journalists who have written acclaimed biographies of Reagan and who have done respected accounts of the history of the cold war. Today, many journalists, like many academics, have stepped back, allowed their emotions and partisan inclinations to cool, and taken a careful look at the record, and they now see Reagan much differently. "Ronald Reagan was not the person that I thought he was when I was covering him in the early 1980s," says *Washington Post* reporter Don Oberdorfer, who has written a book on the period.[7] His is far from an isolated judgment. One could compile a book of positive appraisals of the fortieth president from liberal journalists, ranging from Sam Donaldson to Chris Matthews to Howell Raines. Raines, a White House correspondent for the *New York Times* during the Reagan years, now says, "I think what we need as a nation is another leader on Reagan's scale."[8]

Such a remarkable about-face by the likes of Raines is not atypical. Many longtime Reagan critics, some of the harshest among them, seem to have softened or outright changed. Historian Garry Wills now states,

> Part of Reagan's legacy is what we do *not* see now. We see no Berlin Wall. He said, "Tear down this wall," and it was done. We see no Iron Curtain. In fact, we see no Soviet Union. He called it an Evil Empire, and it evaporated overnight. . . .
>
> Admittedly, Reagan did not accomplish all this by fiat. But it was more than coincidence that the fall began on his watch.[9]

There is hyperbole here, particularly Wills's suggestion of immediate causality. Yet curtains and empires fell, as Reagan expected. It is striking that a Reagan critic like Wills, who once had no respect for Reagan,[10] now grants so much credit.

The most authoritative and critical Reagan biographers, such as Lou Cannon, Richard Reeves, and Edmund Morris—not exactly right-wingers—tend to give him considerable credit, especially for winning the cold war. The view of Reagan has shifted across the board, to the point where he is no longer perceived as a hands-off intellectual lightweight who rarely picked up a pen.

Now, Douglas Brinkley, the editor of *The Reagan Diaries*, tells us his amazement at how much Reagan wrote on a disciplined daily basis as president, fully consistent with the findings of Kiron Skinner, Martin Anderson, and Annelise Anderson in their seminal series of edited volumes on the voluminous writings of Ronald Reagan before and during his presidency—all of which have prompted some to opine, without exaggeration, that Reagan may have the richest, lengthiest record of presidential writings of any chief executive since Thomas Jefferson. That assertion would have blown away the critics in the 1980s, but it is entirely possible that it may be accurate. For the doubting scholar, a perusal of the massive Presidential Handwriting File at the Ronald Reagan Presidential Library would do wonders, beginning with the January 1981 inaugural address that Reagan composed entirely himself—something that modern presidents do not pause to do.

There are even numerous liberal politicians, from Bill Clinton to Ted Kennedy to John Kerry, who now praise Reagan. Kennedy offers the explanation "Reagan will be honored as the president who won the Cold War."[11] Kerry adds, "Perhaps Reagan's greatest monument isn't any building or any structure that bears his name, but it is the absence of the Berlin Wall."[12] The words of Kerry and Kennedy are stunning, given that in the 1980s they excoriated Reagan; their praise today was once unthinkable.

So, again, one could fill a book with encomiums on Reagan from liberal professors, journalists, and politicians. Most compelling, however, is the verdict from one particularly intriguing tribunal: Even former Soviet Communists grant Reagan enormous credit, from *Pravda* and *Izvestia* to Mikhail Gorbachev. Gorbachev called Reagan "a very big person—a very great political leader." At a dinner in Cambridge, England, in 2001, a British academic called Reagan "rather an intellectual lightweight." Gorbachev would not tolerate the slight and reprimanded his host: "You are wrong. President Reagan was a man of real insight, sound political judgment, and courage."[13]

Or take this appraisal from the hard-line Soviet-era publication *Literaturnaya Gazeta*, which informed Soviet citizens at the end of Reagan's presidency, "The years of his presidency have seen an unprecedented surge in America's self-belief, and quite a marked recovery in the economy. . . . Reagan restored America's belief that it is capable of achieving a lot." It closed glowingly, "Reagan is giving America what it has been yearning for. Optimism. Self-belief. Heroes."[14]

Genrikh Trofimenko, head of the Institute for the U.S.A. and Canada Studies of the Russian Academy of Sciences, stated, "Ninety-nine percent of all Russians believe that Reagan won the Cold War."[15]

Herein is a crucial tangential point for students who encounter teachers who claim that Ronald Reagan had nothing to do with ending the cold war. One of my former students, Ashley Falzarano, sent this e-mail to me on July 26, 2007, shortly after her graduation: "Dr. Kengor: I am currently in New Mexico at a conference on the Cold War and how to teach it. Needless to say I am the youngest person here and probably the only one with a conservative bent. You should hear how they talked about Reagan today! It was appalling!"

Those teachers need to know—and their impressionable students need to know—just how far out of the mainstream they are on this subject, not simply in comparison to the wider country and world but even to the much narrower mainstream of academia and media. They are badly under-informed, which is not a sign of good teachers, who need to be, first and foremost, knowledgeable of the most basic realities stemming from the scholarship in their respective fields. They certainly need to have at least a vague understanding of where scholars generally line up on a subject. And yet it is not hyperbole to say that the take on Reagan by many such teachers is literally to the left of Ted Kennedy and *Pravda*.

This may seem like somewhat of a side point on this legacy issue, but it is not: Consider that those teachers will try to make a student like Ashley feel as if her view is part of an isolated, fringe minority. Well, those teachers need to understand that they represent that statistical extreme. Those teachers need to be on the defensive; it is incumbent on them to ascertain and explain why they are swimming against a wide reservoir of bipartisan expert opinion.

THE REAGAN LEGACY BEHIND THE IRON CURTAIN

I would like to give one more example of what I'm talking about; it deals with the perception of Ronald Reagan by those who suffered behind the iron curtain, and specifically in Poland. I will contrast the view of these Poles with the negative judgment of some of those I've encountered in the statistical minority here in America.

Recently, I did a major radio talk show in San Francisco, a very popular one, which I was told was number one in the country in that time slot. The host was a devout Democrat, one who had campaigned for Democrats, and was a voracious reader of presidential history. I was told that he was open-minded, genuine, and very fair. This indeed turned out to be the case. I was impressed. As he proceeded to show me, it was his studious reading of history that brought him to the conclusion that Ronald Reagan was an unusual, remarkable, and highly successful president, especially as related to the cold war. He had read my most recent book on Reagan, which further convinced him, and he invited me on the show to argue with his callers, which I did.

Even I was surprised by what I encountered: angry people who clearly had not read anything on Reagan in two decades. Most astonishing was a caller who informed me that Reagan had nothing to do with ending the cold war but, rather, the people of Poland did; that it was Lech Walesa, Solidarity, and the Polish people who crashed the Soviet empire. This is an astonishing statement. Why? Because Lech Walesa and the whole of the Polish people—in addition to, yes, rightly patting themselves on the back for their enormously influential role in the Soviet downfall—credit Reagan! They say they could not have done it without Reagan. Consider the following examples, drawn from the 1980s, the 1990s, and into today:

In May 1983, the organization Paris Match conducted a poll of six hundred Poles traveling to the West. When asked who was the "last hope" for Poland, the top three figures cited were Pope John Paul II (a native son, of course), the Virgin Mary, and Ronald Reagan (Lech Walesa was fourth, after Reagan).[16]

This thinking was prevalent throughout Poland. Colonel Henryk Piecuch, a high-level official in the Polish Ministry of Internal Affairs in the 1980s, later recalled, "Ronald Reagan was considered a god by some in our country. This pertains especially to the lower ranks of Solidarity."[17]

Journalist Andrew Nagorski was struck by Poles' admiration for Reagan. Nagorski, now a senior editor at *Newsweek*, was Bonn bureau chief for the magazine from 1985 to 1988. He regularly reported from Moscow and Warsaw, and he studied at the University of Krakow. On a visit to Poland in the spring of 1988, when the opposition was dealing daily with riot policy, several Poles wistfully asked Nagorski, "Is it really true that Reagan can't run for a third term?"[18]

In early 1990, the year after the wall fell, Arch Puddington, a journalist who worked for Radio Free Europe, did a series of interviews with Eastern European émigrés and visitors. He asked their opinion of various U.S. presidents. He found that almost all had a highly favorable view of Reagan and his role in the fall of Communism. Puddington said Reagan left a great impression on Poles. One such Pole was Tadeusz Zachurski, who immigrated to the United States in 1981. Zachurski emphasized that Reagan was not only popular among intellectuals but also among the broad masses of Poles, who he said had affectionately dubbed the president "Uncle Reagan." Puddington found that Poles liked Reagan's vitality, sense of humor, and willingness to call a spade a spade. They admired his anti-Soviet rhetoric, particularly the 1983 "evil empire" speech. That explosive remark, as well as the president's prediction that Communism would end up on the "ash heap of history," thrilled Poles. Reagan had spoken their language. Bartak Kaminski, a Polish émigré teaching at the University of Maryland, explained that Reagan was "the first world leader of the post-détente era who was willing to express ideas about the Soviets which were shared by most Poles."[19]

Once victory was theirs, Poles showed their appreciation to Reagan. In September 1990, approaching the first-year postmortem of Communism's collapse in Eastern Europe, Reagan visited Gdansk, home of the shipyard in which Solidarity was born. The former president received what both United Press International and Reuters described as a "hero's welcome." Despite a torrential rain and punishing hail, seven thousand braved the storm to greet Reagan in front of the shipyard gate. They sang "Sto Lat" (May He Live One Hundred Years), a Polish anthem sung only to honor the nation's heroes. They chanted "Thank you, thank you!" In a gesture Reagan must have loved, Lech Walesa's parish priest handed him a sword and explained, "I am giving you the saber for helping us to chop off the head of communism."[20] In turn, Reagan told them, "You have triggered fast changes in the political map of Central and Eastern Europe." Referring to the other dominoes that subsequently fell, Reagan said, "One might say that [this] was the shipyard that launched a half-dozen revolutions."[21]

An ongoing powerful testimony to Poles' credit to Reagan has been the modern movement inside Poland to name things after him. "I will not rest until there is a Ronald Reagan Square in Warsaw," says Radek Sikorski, former deputy minister of foreign affairs and minister of defense for today's free Poland. The holdup has been Polish law, which states that public places cannot be named after people until they have been dead for at least five years. "We want some major form of commemoration," says Sikorski. "They [Poles] at least want a Reagan statue in a place of significance."[22] Precisely that was proposed by a committee of Poles called the Ronald Reagan Legacy Committee. Sikorski is chair of the committee, which includes Polish cabinet members, members of Parliament, and major Solidarity figures.

Still, Poles have done what they can. Reagan was made an honorary citizen of Gdansk and Krakow, the cities where the Solidarity tradition was strongest. Separately, a competition was held to choose a name for a square in front of a train station in Warsaw. No suggested names were listed. The public voted. Naturally, the winner was the architect who constructed the train station. Ronald Reagan, however, was runner-up.

This sentiment rose to the very top. Lech Walesa hailed Reagan's impact, stating in May 1996, "His policy supporting the freedom movement in Central and Eastern Europe provided [Solidarity] with a very strong backing." He praised Reagan's devotion to "a few simple rules: human rights, democracy, freedom of speech . . . and his conviction that it is not the people who are there for the sake of the state, but that the state is there for the sake of the citizens."[23] Reagan had indeed said exactly this many times, and apparently Walesa listened. Walesa once said to Reagan, "We stood on the two sides of the artificially erected wall. Solidarity broke down this wall from the Eastern side and on the Western side it was you. . . . Your decisiveness and resolve were for us a hope and help in the most difficult moments."[24]

Poles had needed a friend, said Walesa, "and such was Ronald Reagan." He said Reagan challenged rather than avoided problems and was "favored by the muse" of history; that muse liked Reagan "so much" that she whispered in his ear and told him what to do. "We owe so much to Ronald Reagan," concluded Walesa. "We Poles owe him freedom." Teary-eyed, he said Reaganesquely, "God bless America."[25]

As recently as April 2005, Walesa told me that Reagan had "emboldened" and "encouraged" him in the 1980s. He spoke of Reagan's "testimony to the truth and liberty" and "his understanding of life as living in light without a lie," which "was always an inspiration for me." Walesa's words were translated by Tomasz Pompowski, a senior editor and reporter at *Fakt,* the largest newspaper in Poland. As he translated, Pompowski could not help but add that Reagan had meant a "great deal" to him as well.[26]

There are now formal plans to erect a statue to Reagan in the center of Warsaw. Also, in July 2007, Polish president Lech Kaczynski flew to California to present Nancy Reagan with a posthumous award for her husband: the Order of the White Eagle, the nation's highest political honor.

While there are many reasons for this remarkable record, for this enduring legacy of success, it is, again, Ronald Reagan's cold war achievement—now widely attributed to more than luck—that heads the list. Indeed, I would assert that the debate now, throughout even academia and journalism, is not over whether Reagan contributed to the end of the cold war but to what degree. The debate hinges largely on the credit that Reagan should share with the likes of Mikhail Gorbachev, Margaret Thatcher, Lech Walesa, Vaclav Havel, and Pope John Paul II.

In a way, after winning the presidency by taking forty-four of fifty states against the incumbent in 1980 and forty-nine of fifty against a challenger in 1984—in the latter, he swept the Electoral College by a count of 525 to 13—Reagan never looked back. When this man ran for the presidency, there was no need to recount Florida—which brings us to George W. Bush.

Bush's Burden

I note all of this, admittedly at great length, for two reasons: First, it demonstrates the fact of and reasons for Ronald Reagan's enormous popularity throughout his presidency and to this day, which is fundamental to the question of his legacy. Second, it underscores that Reagan has left behind some awfully large shoes for a modern president to try to fill, especially for the first two-term Republican since Reagan, one likewise seeking to spread freedom around the world: President Bush. For George W. Bush, this is not a legacy but an albatross—a burden.

When compared to Reagan, Bush is often found lacking. Of course, to be sure, Bush is hardly alone in that regard. Reagan's success is all the more notable when juxtaposed to his contemporaries. Few even among Reagan's two-term contemporaries won the Electoral College by combined margins of 1,014 to 62.

Dating back to Lyndon Johnson, modern presidencies had ended in despair. LBJ, who replaced a president who was killed in office, was destroyed by Vietnam and decided not to pursue reelection. His successor, Richard Nixon, resigned in disgrace and suffered mental and physical repercussions. The uninspiring Gerald Ford was unable to win an election. Jimmy Carter's presidency was vigorously rejected in 1980; to this day, one senses his feeling of rejection.

In the other direction, prior to Eisenhower, Harry Truman left office with an approval rating that plummeted to near 20 percent. He called the White House the "Great White Jail." Only today has history recognized his greatness. Among other twentieth-century presidents, the job took a toll on Herbert Hoover, Warren Harding, Calvin Coolidge, and William Howard Taft; it ruined Woodrow Wilson mentally and physically. FDR died in office.

Unlike many predecessors, Reagan was not destroyed by the presidency. George H. W. Bush, as Reagan's vice president, recalled that in eight years he never once heard Reagan complain of the "loneliness of his job."[27] Bush remembered how Lloyd Cutler during the Carter years had written that the job had become too much for one man and that maybe it was time for a parliamentary system in the United States. "Well," declared Bush, "that was before Ronald Reagan came along."[28]

The odds against Reagan were great, making their reversal under Reagan all the greater. He made the presidency look easy. Lest anyone think his taking over the helm coincided with a lucky reversal in a trend, Reagan's handpicked successor, who won primarily because he was Reagan's handpicked successor, won only one term, and the president who finished the century, Bill Clinton, was impeached.

So George W. Bush is not all alone in a corner. Or is he? Well, at certain points in his presidency, he indeed was alone, at the bottom, among his contemporaries. A December 2006 Gallup poll found that Americans considered George W. Bush the most unsuccessful of modern presidents, even lower than Carter and Nixon, the two chief executives usually counted on to bring up the bottom. Whom did Americans judge the most popular? You guessed it: Ronald Reagan. That same Gallup poll tallied 64 percent of respondents judging Reagan outstanding or above average and only 10 percent rating him below average or poor. This was yet another affirmation of the response to Reagan today, consistent with an extraordinary June 2005 survey by the Discovery Channel and AOL

(2.4 million participants) that declared Reagan the "greatest American of all time," beating Lincoln and Washington. Other surveys, like a 2001 Gallup poll, showed that Americans rank Reagan the greatest president of all time.[29]

BUSH'S UNPOPULARITY

We could do an entire seminar simply exploring the various reasons for George W. Bush's failed popularity. That said, few would dare doubt that his perceived foreign policy failures—kind of the anti-Reagan—played the principal role. And yet it certainly did not start that way.

Through the first eight months of his presidency, George W. Bush enjoyed impressive popularity, striking in light of the extremely divisive 2000 presidential contest. It is often forgotten how quickly public opinion turned in his favor. Even before the inauguration in January 2001, *Time* magazine stepped up to name Bush its 2000 person of the year. *Time* wrote of the new president, "Even Democrats now say privately that Bush and his soft serums may be better suited [than Gore] to cure the disease that afflicts the capital."[30] The perception of Bush as a unifier was a key motivation for *Time*.[31] This thinking was captured in the sentiments of Richard Cohen, a liberal columnist for the *Washington Post* who had voted for Gore but then soon changed his preference: "I now think that under current circumstances he [Gore] would not be the right man for the presidency. If I could, I would withdraw my vote." He said that Bush's claim to be a unifier rather than a divider was not just campaign talk—"In Bush's case it appears to be true." Gore, on the other hand, wrote Cohen, had "little" such ability.[32]

It was "so far, so good" for Bush. And that popularity suddenly soared even higher immediately after September 11, 2001, and in the days that followed. Recall that great moment on September 14, when Bush flew to New York to meet with grieving families and with those digging for corpses amid the immense pile of concrete, steel, ash, and flesh at Ground Zero.[33] He toured the site of the impact. At 4:40 PM, at the corner of Murray and West streets, he paused to say a few words. He stood atop the rubble, wrapped his left arm around a firefighter, grabbed a bullhorn, and began shouting. A rescue worker heckled good-naturedly, "Can't hear you." Bush yelled back, to laughter, "I can't go any louder." The wise guy New Yorker pushed again, "I can't hear you." To thunderous applause, Bush replied, "I can hear you. I can hear you. The rest of the world hears you. And the people who knocked down these buildings will hear all of us soon." The rescue workers responded by chanting, "U.S.A.! U.S.A.! U.S.A.!"[34]

It was a powerful, patriotic, and impromptu moment. Those on the scene loved it. America loved it. Bush's staff later called it the defining moment of his presidency.

America was weepy, but Bush's statement helped pick up the nation from its knees. The bullhorn was like Uncle Sam's clenched, shaking fist, warning that justice would soon be served. That day, an ABC News poll registered Bush with an 86 percent approval rating. A week later, a *Newsweek* poll found that 89 percent of the public approved of his handling of the crisis, and a *Newsweek* article comparing him to FDR said Bush had found his "true voice."[35] That approval number actually rose even higher, and held above 90 percent, as the president initiated a superbly executed removal of the Taliban in Afghanistan through November 2001.

This striking height of approval and popularity largely held through late 2002 and into early 2003. So what happened? When did the approval begin to decline? The answer: Bush's sun set when he began pushing for war in Iraq in late 2002 and early 2003, and it did a free fall as the body bags stacked up during the occupation in the years that followed.

In light of that fact, maybe the most inexplicable, unthoughtful assertion ever directed at the entire Bush presidency came in 2003 from Democratic senator Ted Kennedy of Massachusetts, who publicly contended that George W. Bush pursued war in Iraq for political purposes: "This was made up in Texas," said Kennedy, "announced . . . to the Republican leadership that war was going to take place and was going to be good politically."[36] Quite the contrary, at the moment Bush decided to pursue a highly risky path to war, he was still surfing an unprecedented wave of popularity. Political scientists speak of the rally-round-the-flag phenomenon—a boost that presidents receive during national tragedy. Typically, this lift lasts a few weeks, at best a few months. Yet Bush's post–September 11 jump lasted over a year—the longest rally-round-the-flag peak ever recorded. And he gave it up to go to war. He sacrificed political fortune for what he thought was right. He never regained that post–September 11 upsurge. Moreover, at the time of Kennedy's comment, Bush and his staff fully understood that if body bags piled up in Iraq, he faced the prospect of being a one-term president. Kennedy's assertion was not only completely unfair but utterly nonsensical.

On this peak and valley, I find it almost poetic that while Bush was considering and preparing the country for war in Iraq, he was doing two daily morning readings: the Bible and a book of daily devotionals by the late theologian Oswald Chambers, titled *My Utmost for His Highest.* In that book, Chambers wrote that the "true test" of spiritual life comes in exhibiting the power to descend from the mountaintop. "If we have only the power to go up," he wrote, "something is wrong."[37] Well, in pursuing war, Bush willingly chose to descend the mountaintop of public opinion he reached after September 11—he did so to do what he felt, correctly or not, was the right thing, not the political thing.

Bush never reclaimed that peak; it vanished for the remainder of his presidency. The ups and then downs, the latter of which continued slower and longer and more pronounced, and with vitriol and bile from his detractors, contributed to a pall over Bush's popularity. The pall seemed permanent as the death toll in Iraq rose well after the remarkably successful invasion and removal of Saddam Hussein—that is, during the postwar period of reconstruction. There remains a direct correlation between the rise in body bags containing dead American soldiers and the decline in Bush's approval contained in opinion polls.

Bush Measured against Reagan

Because of that bitter, increasingly costly war in Iraq, Americans questioned the forty-third president's leadership more than ever before, and George W. Bush watched his approval ratings plummet to all-time lows.

Now, that said, such challenging times were known by past presidents—including the best of them, even those that America honors during Presidents' Day: Washington and Lincoln led their nation to victory in wars that threatened to rip apart their country. Another president who sought to lead America to victory in a difficult war likewise persevered—Ronald Reagan. And it is Reagan's cold war triumph that underscores notable differences as well as interesting parallels—and, alas on the positive side, maybe even some inspiration—for George W. Bush's struggles in the War on Terror. These comparisons hold some key lessons for Bush's detractors.

On the one hand, consider the differences.

Obviously, Bush lacks Reagan's communication skills and ability to disarm political opponents with gentle wit. This has enabled his opponents to define public perception of his handling of the war, in a way Reagan's critics could not. Bush simply does not have Reagan's prime-time television charm or the ability to appeal to Americans in the same persuasive, winsome manner.

Also, comparisons between the two presidents are often unfair because of vastly divergent circumstances: The Soviets did not directly attack us, as did the terrorists; we never engaged the USSR in a hot war. And because the Soviets embraced an atheistic ideology, they feared death, not believing in eternal rewards. Quite the contrary, the radical Islamic enemy views death in the name of Allah as a ticket to paradise. For Bush, that is a more dangerous enemy—one that cannot be permitted to acquire nuclear weapons. Moreover, Reagan, who spent a lifetime preparing to defeat Soviet Communism, could win the cold war by changing one country, the USSR. Bush, who prior to his presidency never imagined what history had in store for him, cannot win the War on Terror by changing one country.

On the other hand, there are key common positive aspects in Bush and Reagan.

Most significant among them, even Republicans have failed to grasp the most important shared objective of the two presidents: Bush stated explicitly that he was seeking to carry on Reagan's "march of freedom," a march that was begun centuries ago, not months ago—and that conservatives saluted when Reagan announced the goal in his historic 1982 Westminster address. Against great odds, Bush attempted to shift Reagan's march of freedom to that one area where it has been most resistant but is most needed—the Middle East.[38]

This is not to say that Ronald Reagan would have supported the decision to invade Iraq. That is impossible to know. At the least, however, Reagan would commend Bush's goal of expanding freedom and—ever the optimist—would most likely be hopeful.

What are the lessons for Bush from Reagan?

Perhaps most significant, Reagan found nonmilitaristic means to defeat the enemy, from extremely bold forms of economic warfare to other methods, such as aiding forces resisting the Soviets on various fronts. Reagan was able to marshal a multitude of resources that enabled him to pull off what no one ten years earlier judged possible: he defeated the Soviet Union and won the cold war without expending thousands of American lives. George W. Bush lost thousands of precious lives and, in the process, was unable to convince America that victory was in sight.

In the spring of 2007, I did a four-part series of articles for Townhall.com, in which I detailed three cases where Reagan defeated the enemy without firing a shot—from the pursuit of extraordinary examples of clandestine economic warfare to aiding underground freedom fighters like Lech Walesa's Solidarity movement in Poland. That series got a lot of attention. People (especially conservatives) desperately wanted to know how Reagan did this without going to war, without Americans getting killed—a question of intense curiosity in light of those casualty reports coming in regularly from Iraq.

BUSH, REAGAN, AND THE USE OF FORCE

Picking up that thought, I believe that only recently, under the glare of the high death toll in Iraq, has it become clear to most Americans how rarely Ronald Reagan used military force. Despite his hawkish reputation, Reagan was quite restrained in pulling the trigger, and he did so only rarely; he understood that the few occasions in which he dispatched troops had to be successful, with little bloodshed.

Generally, I would say that it is greatly unappreciated how seldom the tough-talking Reagan chose to use force. For instance, he deployed troops in combat far fewer times than Bill Clinton, not to mention other presidents. In the few cases where he used force, action was fast and decisive, largely successful, and usually a morale booster. Charles W. Dunn notes that this rapid, rare use of force allowed Reagan to avoid liberal criticism over the use of excessive force in the battle against Communism. He chose prudently, selecting spots that were eminently doable.[39]

Agreeing that Reagan was "very reluctant to use power," contrary to his trigger-happy cowboy image, former Reagan aide Kenneth Adelman offers an instructive example: Secretary of State Al Haig, according to Adelman, underwent "tremendous agony" the first two years of the administration because "he wanted to take it to the source and go after Cuba," but Reagan vetoed the idea. Adelman explained, "Basically because Ronald Reagan, whenever he used force, wanted to make it pretty easy, pretty cheap, pretty quick, and pretty decisive. . . . [He was] quite moderate, and quite unwilling to really use much."[40]

Reagan felt force was necessary to settle scores—but not all scores at all times. He felt that one must recognize not only force's authority but also its limitations.

The two cases of Reagan's using force were quite limited: one was the strike against Libya's Muammar el-Qaddafi in April 1986, and the other was the invasion of Grenada in October 1983. Grenada holds some telling lessons for the diverging reactions to the Reagan and Bush presidencies.

On October 25, 1983, some five thousand U.S. troops stormed the Caribbean island of Grenada, where renegade Marxists had murdered Prime Minister Maurice Bishop. A violent Marxist military council trained by Cuba put itself in charge, shot and jailed Bishop supporters, enacted martial law, and imposed a shoot-on-sight, twenty-four-hour curfew that threatened all those living on the island, including roughly one thousand Americans, seven hundred of whom were students at St. George's University School of Medicine.

Ronald Reagan dubbed Grenada a "communist power grab." His administration believed that the USSR and Cuba were building military installations on the island, including a landing strip, and stockpiling materiel. They later found an enormous cache of weapons, armored vehicles, and military patrol boats, enough to equip thousands of troops. This included 10,000 assault rifles, 4,500 submachine guns, 11.5 million rounds of ammunition, 294 portable rocket launchers with 16,000 rockets, 15,000 hand grenades, 7,000 land mines, 23,000 uniforms, and much more. During battle, U.S. troops engaged roughly eight hundred Cuban soldiers.

To Reagan, Grenada posed the hazard of not only a joint military installation orchestrated by Moscow and Havana but also another full-fledged "Cuba" operating in the Western Hemisphere. Reagan was already committed to ceding "not one inch" of territory to Communism anywhere, least of all in America's backyard, where he already feared Communism in Nicaragua and El Salvador.

The October 25 excursion became the largest U.S. military operation since Vietnam. The intervention was also an emotional victory for the post-Watergate, postmalaise, Vietnam-syndrome America: a shot in the arm to U.S. morale. A startlingly quick thirty hours after the start of the "rescue mission" (as Reagan called it), the first evacuated medical student to debark the airplane dropped to his knees and kissed the tarmac as he touched the safety of the soil of Charleston, South Carolina. It was the sort of smiling military triumph that had become sadly unfamiliar to Americans.

Yet here is the crucial point for my purposes in this chapter: There were remarkably few casualties, particularly when measured against what Americans had experienced a decade earlier. Only nineteen died, with a little over one hundred wounded. By comparison, the United States lost fifty-eight thousand in Vietnam. The commander of the task force in Grenada, Vice Admiral Joseph Metcalf III, rightly boasted, "We blew them away."

Now, that said, what is easily forgotten, and what I alluded to earlier, is the fact that Reagan had less support for going to war in Grenada than George W. Bush did in going to war in Iraq twenty years later—or, I should clarify, less initial support.

Whereas Americans supported the Grenada attack, it was lambasted by the international community. Even Reagan's buddy Margaret Thatcher opposed him; she shouted at him on the telephone in the most disapproving tone and language she ever directed at her friend; in other words, Reagan didn't even have Britain's backing. The vote at the UN Security Council was 11 to 1 against the United States, while the General Assembly vote was 108 to 9, with America joined only by El Salvador, Israel, and the six Caribbean neighbors that requested U.S. assistance in the first place.

When George W. Bush went to war in Iraq in 2003, he initially had far more support than Ronald Reagan had with the Grenada intervention. Despite the irresponsible statements by Bush detractors calling the Iraq war a "unilateral" effort by the United States, the fact was that a remarkable coalition had been forged. By March 18, 2003, shortly before the invasion, Secretary of State Colin Powell announced a U.S.-led coalition of thirty to forty-five nations[41]—one not only larger than the huge 1991 Gulf War coalition but, in fact, one of the biggest military coalitions in all history. The coalition included Afghanistan, Australia, Britain, Czech Republic, Hungary, Italy, Japan, Lithuania, Netherlands, Poland, South Korea, Spain, and dozens of others.[42] Such a multilateral stamp of approval was precisely what critics had clamored for. And the fact that it included a nation once run by the Taliban, and once Osama bin Laden's home, was extraordinary.

Bush's international support was buoyed by opinion polls at home. Polls showed that by March 2003 the public, though initially luke-warm—and despite some massive protests in major cities in the United States and around the world—strongly supported Bush, usually by a margin of 70 to 20 percent.[43]

Thus Bush arguably had stronger initial support for his interven-tion in Iraq than Reagan did in Grenada. So why did Bush eventually plummet in the polls because of the war in Iraq whereas Reagan never dropped—and only rose—after the war in Grenada? Because, as Dunn noted, Reagan's use of force was quick and successful, with minimal ca-sualties. Reagan's intervention was over in days, not years, with fewer than a couple dozen killed rather than thousands.

FAITH AND HISTORY

So, on this rare occasion when he used military force, Reagan likewise encountered strong international disapproval. Yet, like Bush later, he withstood the opposition. And he did so in part by drawing on some-thing worth underscoring here: Like Bush, Reagan relied on a deep faith in God, in country, and in his visions for America and the world. For both leaders, their self-confidence gave them remarkable perseverance in the face of harsh criticism—criticism we have conveniently forgotten in Reagan's case. More crucial, their faith in God was the bedrock of that unbending confidence. Reagan was sure that America was blessed by a divine Providence who had a divine plan for the United States, a plan that, said Reagan, quoting his mother, "always worked for the best."

George W. Bush, despite extreme perceptions of what he does and does not believe,[44] has been a bit more circumspect about what he be-lieves God desires for America, though he is certain that God has a plan for his country, his world, and himself and that it is God that guides his-tory. He said he could not be president if he did not believe in a "divine plan that supersedes all human plans."[45] Before the inauguration, the president-elect sat for an interview with *Time.* "I believe things happen for a reason," he said of the messy election that made him president. "It is a unique moment, and I intend to seize it. . . . I view it as a very posi-tive opportunity."[46]

God, Bush is sure, will chart his ultimate course, even while he, as president, laid out his own vision. Plan as he might, he is at God's mercy, and that reassures him.[47] This trust in God's guidance is in part what Bush means when he says he is still growing spiritually. Many people talk about faith, but Bush is walking by faith. "I also recognize that a walk is a walk," he says; "it's a never-ending journey."[48] When his evangelical supporters hail him for "walking the walk," they may not know the full degree to which that is the case.

As the invasion of Iraq approached in 2003, the pressure on Bush was acute. Some questioned his very faith, his very understanding of God. Just a few weeks before the first Tomahawks were unleashed, he spoke to a packed room at the National Prayer Breakfast at the Washington Hilton. He acknowledged those fellow spiritual warriors who were present and spoke of the current challenge and time of "testing." He talked of how he appreciated the prayer he felt from the nation. At 8:20 AM, he ended his brief remarks with this common anthem: "We can . . . be confident in the ways of Providence, even when they are far from our understanding. Events aren't moved by blind change and chance. Behind all of life and all of history, there's a dedication and purpose, set by the hand of a just and faithful God. . . . We pray for wisdom to know and do what is right."[49]

As he said in his first presidential inaugural address, "We are not this story's author, who fills time and eternity with His purpose. Yet His purpose is achieved in our duty." God is the "Author" of history, says Bush, with a measure of reassurance. Ronald Reagan had that same sense, which likewise always reassured him with an identical, unshakable, faith-based confidence.[50]

Having said all of this, comparisons between Ronald Reagan and George W. Bush are often unfair because of the uniqueness and gravity of President Bush's challenge. Consider that Reagan became president four decades into the cold war, whereas Bush was the first post–September 11 president; thus Bush presided over the start of a long War on Terror, not its finish. We should no more have expected victory from Bush at this point in the war than we expected it from Harry Truman in 1947. Bush seems to have reconciled himself to this essential reality.

Alas, then, perhaps the ultimate contrast in the two men could be the most bittersweet for Bush: Reagan was blessed to be able to enjoy the fruits of his labors in his lifetime, and before his mind was robbed of its memories by Alzheimer's disease—he watched the Berlin Wall fall the year he left the presidency, and the USSR collapsed two years later.

To the contrary, Bush acknowledged that if he was vindicated in the Middle East, his vindication would not happen while he was president. In fact, he did not expect the changes to take place until he left this earth. Bush himself wryly noted this in an October 2005 speech honoring—you guessed it—Ronald Reagan. The forty-third president seemed a bit envious.

In that speech, George W. Bush said that Reagan recognized "that America has always prevailed by standing firmly on principles and never backing down in the face of evil." He said that Reagan understood that the struggles America faces are "a test of wills and ideas, a trial of spiritual resolve." Invoking Reagan, Bush claimed, "And like the ideology of communism, Islamic radicalism is doomed to fail." Prevailing, Bush insisted, will require following Reagan's example of leadership, strategy, vision, and "resolve to stay in the fight until the fight [is] won."[51]

For now, George W. Bush must be content with leaving the presidency an unpopular president—like Harry Truman. Yet, he committed himself to not exiting the presidency without trying to meet his goals in the War on Terror. Like Reagan, coincidentally, it was an unwavering faith-based confidence that allowed him to persevere.

Finally, I dare to say that not only is George W. Bush eclipsed by Reagan's shadow, but, as we saw over and over again in the Republican presidential debates for the 2008 nomination, so were the contenders, as they vied to see who was most like Ronald Reagan. But, then, that is another issue, and another burden for someone else—albeit the same Reagan legacy.

Notes

1. On these sources, see Paul Kengor, "Reagan among the Professors," *Policy Review*, December 1999–January 2000, 15–27, and Paul Kengor, "The Legacy of Ronald Reagan: The Academic View" (lecture at the Conference on the Reagan Presidency, Saint Vincent College, Latrobe, PA, October 10, 2001).

This is not to imply that all of these sources hail Reagan across the board, but only to observe that they have treated him with fairness and have commended him and his presidency for various reasons, and often unexpectedly. For instance, James T. Patterson, a liberal, has been quite critical of certain Reagan domestic policies. On the other hand, John Sloan, also a liberal, has praised Reagan generously and personally rates him a "near-great" president. See John W. Sloan, review of *The Reagan Presidency: Pragmatic Conservatism and Its*

Legacies, ed. W. Elliot Brownlee and Hugh Davis Graham, *Presidential Studies Quarterly,* December 2004, 909–10.

2. See Hugh Heclo, "Ronald Reagan and the American Public Philosophy," in *The Reagan Presidency: Pragmatic Conservatism and Its Legacies,* ed. W. Elliot Brownlee and Hugh Davis Graham (Lawrence: University Press of Kansas, 2003).

3. In his seminal work, *The United States and the End of the Cold War,* in the chapter titled, "The Unexpected Ronald Reagan," Gaddis maintains that the president succeeded in "bringing about the most significant improvement in Soviet-American relations since the end of World War II." While he grants much of the credit to Mikhail Gorbachev's receptivity, Gaddis asserts, "It would be a mistake to credit him [Gorbachev] solely with the responsibility for what happened: Ronald Reagan deserves a great deal of the credit as well." Gaddis has urged colleagues to put aside "preconceptions" in evaluating the Reagan record. John Lewis Gaddis, *The United States and the End of the Cold War: Implications, Reconsiderations, Provocations* (New York: Oxford University Press, 1992), 130–31. Also see John Lewis Gaddis, "The Tragedy of Cold War History," *Foreign Affairs* 73, no. 1 (1994): 148, and John Lewis Gaddis, "Hanging Tough Paid Off," *Bulletin of the Atomic Scientists,* January–February 1989, 11.

4. See James MacGregor Burns, "Risks of the Middle," *Washington Post,* October 24, 1999.

5. See "Historians Presidential Leadership Survey," *C-SPAN,* http://www.c-span.org/PresidentialSurvey/Index.aspx.

6. See "Hail to the Chief," *WSJ.com,* http://www.opinionjournal.com/hail/.

7. "Discussant: Don Oberdorfer," in *President Reagan and the World,* ed. Eric J. Schmertz, Natalie Datlof, and Alexej Ugrinsky (Westport, CT: Greenwood Press, 1997), 129.

8. On Raines's switch, see Howell Raines, "The 'Dumb' Factor," *Washington Post,* August 27, 2004, and David A. Andelman, "Life after the *Times,*" *Forbes,* May 17, 2006. These are juxtaposed in Lou Cannon and Carl M. Cannon, *Reagan's Disciple: George W. Bush's Troubled Quest for a Presidential Legacy* (New York: Public Affairs, 2008), 28.

9. Garry Wills, *Reagan's America: Innocents at Home* (Garden City, NY: Doubleday, 1987), xv.

10. Among other examples, see ibid., xi.

11. Kennedy quoted in Ted Anthony, "U.S. and the World Mourn Reagan's Death," Associated Press, June 5, 2004. Kennedy's statement was also posted on the website of the Ronald Reagan Presidential Foundation and Library, http://www.reaganfoundation.org/.

12. Kerry quoted in Cannon and Cannon, *Reagan's Disciple,* 53.

13. Jack F. Matlock Jr., *Reagan and Gorbachev: How the Cold War Ended* (New York: Random House, 2004), 326. Matlock attended the dinner.

14. Vladimir Simonov, "Political Portrait of Ronald Reagan," *Literaturnaya Gazeta*, May 25, 1988, 14, printed as "Weekly Presents 'Political Portrait' of Reagan," FBIS-SOV-88-102, May 26, 1988, 8, 10.

15. "Discussant: Genrikh Aleksandrovich (Henry) Trofimenko," in Schmertz, Datlof, and Ugrinsky, *President Reagan and the World*, 134–45, esp. 138.

16. These poll results are reprinted in Teresa Rakowska-Harmstone, "Communist Regimes' Psychological Warfare against Their Societies: The Case of Poland," in *Psychological Operations and Political Warfare in Long-Term Strategic Planning*, ed. Janos Radvanyi (New York: Praeger, 1990), 103.

17. Piecuch quoted in Peter Schweizer, *Reagan's War: The Epic Story of His Forty Year Struggle and Final Triumph over Communism* (New York: Doubleday, 2002), 236.

18. Andrew Nagorski, "Reagan Had It Right," *Newsweek*, October 21, 2002, 68.

19. Arch Puddington, "Voices in the Wilderness: The Western Heroes of Eastern Europe," *Policy Review*, Summer 1990, 34–35.

20. Maciek Gajewski, "In Solidarity's Cradle, Poles Applaud Reagan," United Press International, September 16, 1990; "Poles Give Reagan a Hero's Welcome," Reuters, September 16, 1990.

21. Gajewski, "In Solidarity's Cradle." Reagan's response, of course, was a play on the face of Helen of Troy, which launched a thousand ships.

22. Radek Sikorski, interview by the author, February 28, March 3, 2003.

23. Lech Walesa, speech at Reagan Legacy conference (Ronald Reagan Presidential Library, Simi Valley, CA, May 20, 1996). See Mack Reed, "Walesa Hails Reagan at Daylong Seminar," *Los Angeles Times*, May 21, 1996, A1, A18.

24. Walesa quoted in John O'Sullivan, "Friends at Court," *National Review*, May 27, 1991, 4. For his part, Reagan called Walesa a heroic figure. Ronald Reagan, remarks on signing the Human Rights Day, Bill of Rights Day, and Human Rights Week Proclamation (Washington, DC, December 8, 1988), Public Papers of President Ronald W. Reagan, Ronald Reagan Presidential Library, http://www.reagan.utexas.edu/archives/speeches/publicpapers.html.

25. Walesa, speech.

26. Lech Walesa, interview by the author, April 25, 2005.

27. George H. W. Bush, conversation with the author, Erie, PA, June 30, 2004. "I learned *so much* from him," Bush said of Reagan. "He taught me *everything* about politics. He meant so much to me."

28. Bush quoted in Edmund Morris, *Dutch: A Memoir of Ronald Reagan* (New York: Random House, 1999), 650.

29. See Cannon and Cannon, *Reagan's Disciple*, xii.

30. Nancy Gibbs, "Person of the Year: George W. Bush," *Time,* December 17, 2000.

31. See comments by Walter Isaacson on NBC's *Meet the Press with Tim Russert,* December 17, 2000.

32. Richard Cohen, "Gore Can't Heal the Hurt," *Washington Post,* November 24, 2000.

33. Bill Sammon, *Fighting Back: The War on Terrorism from inside the Bush White House* (Washington, DC: Regnery, 2002), 193–94.

34. George W. Bush, remarks to police, firemen, and rescue workers at the World Trade Center site (New York City, September 14, 2001), American Presidency Project, University of California, Santa Barbara, http://www.presidency.ucsb.edu/ (hereafter cited as Presidency Project).

35. Howard Fineman, "A President Finds His True Voice," *Newsweek,* September 24, 2001.

36. Kennedy made this remark on September 18, 2003. For a stinging response, see Charles Krauthammer, "Ted Kennedy, Losing It," *Washington Post,* September 26, 2003, A27.

37. Oswald Chambers, *My Utmost for His Highest,* devotions for October 1, 4.

38. See Paul Kengor, "The 'March of Freedom' from Reagan to Bush," *Policy Review,* December 2007–January 2008.

39. See Charles W. Dunn, *The Scarlet Thread of Scandal: Morality and the American Presidency* (Lanham, MD: Rowman Littlefield, 2000), 150.

40. "Discussant: Kenneth L. Adelman," in Schmertz, Datlof, and Ugrinsky, *President Reagan and the World,* 240.

41. The number depended on the level of support, which ranged from vocal and open (thirty nations) to more quiet and discreet (fifteen nations).

42. "Powell: 30 Nations in Coalition," Associated Press, March 18, 2003.

43. For instance, a March 11–12, 2003, Fox News/Opinion Dynamics poll showed 71 percent supporting the use of U.S. military force to disarm Hussein and 20 percent opposing it.

44. See Paul Kengor, "What Bush Believes," *New York Times,* October 18, 2004.

45. George W. Bush, president's radio address, April 14, 2001, Presidency Project; George W. Bush, *A Charge to Keep* (New York: Morrow, 1999), 6.

46. Bush quoted in Gibbs, "Person of the Year."

47. "Our faith teaches us that while weeping may endure for a night, joy comes in the morning," says Bush. "And while faith will not make our path easy, it will give us strength for the journey ahead." George W. Bush, remarks via satellite to the 2002 Southern Baptist Convention (June 11, 2002), Presidency Project.

48. George W. Bush, interview by Steven Waldman, October 2000, quoted at http://www.beliefnet.com/News/Politics/2000/07/A-Library-Of-Quotations-On-Religion-And-Politics-By-George-W-Bush.aspx.

49. George W. Bush, remarks at the National Prayer Breakfast (Washington, DC, February 6, 2003), Presidency Project.

50. On this, see my two works *God and Ronald Reagan: A Spiritual Life* (New York: HarperCollins, 2004) and *God and George W. Bush: A Spiritual Life* (New York: HarperCollins, 2004).

51. George W. Bush, remarks at the ribbon-cutting ceremony for the Air Force One Pavilion (Ronald Reagan Presidential Library, Simi Valley, CA, October 21, 2005), Presidency Project.

THREE DECADES OF REAGANISM

Andrew E. Busch

It is a formidable task to assess the legacy of any president. Ronald Reagan presents particular challenges, including lack of historical distance and the consequent connection of Reagan to ongoing disputes and partisan agendas. Indeed, during the 2008 presidential campaign, Reagan's legacy was bandied about as a political football. Presidential greatness, for which Reagan contends, can be gauged in so many ways and affords so many potential thresholds for greatness that it is hard to imagine a consensus forming on any but a tiny handful of truly indispensable presidents, perhaps only Washington and Lincoln. Nevertheless, it is possible to offer a draft answer to the question.

REAGAN'S REPUTATION TRAJECTORY

The place to start—though certainly not the place to finish—is by examining the trajectory of Reagan's reputation, and how that trajectory compares with the other dominant president of the twentieth century, Franklin Delano Roosevelt. Reputation is necessarily attached to greatness but is not sufficient evidence of it. There may be some less than great presidents who are nonetheless beloved, but one is hard pressed to think of an arguably great president who is not beloved.

When Reagan left office, it was clear that he was enormously popular among ordinary Americans. In a January 1989 CBS News/*New York Times* poll, 68 percent said they approved of the job Reagan had done since 1981. A small movement was even launched with the aim of adding Reagan's face to Mount Rushmore. However, the political opposition, including elements of the media and intellectual worlds, did not immediately accommodate themselves to Reagan's reputation among the people and instead went to work attempting to undermine it. This resulted in frequent commentary highlighting Reagan's alleged contribution to AIDS, the savings and loan crisis, homelessness, and a variety of other social and economic ills. A poll of historians, spearheaded by Arthur M. Schlesinger Jr., was released in the mid-1990s placing Reagan in the "below average" category among America's presidents. While adopting some conservative themes like support for welfare reform and the death penalty, Bill Clinton claimed in his 1992 presidential campaign, "For the last twelve years, we have been in the grip of a failed economic theory." Some observers wrote an epitaph for Reaganism, and implicitly for Reagan's legacy, when Clinton's victory seemed to suggest a national repudiation of Reagan's economic policies.

However, within two years the tables had turned again when Clinton's two-year-long experiment in revivifying the Great Society collapsed. Reagan was increasingly likely to be rated highly by academics, either in group surveys or, as Paul Kengor observed in 1999, in individual works. Politically, Republicans continued to attach themselves to Reagan vigorously (and, in losing years, desperately); every presidential campaign began with those seeking the GOP nomination claiming to be the real heir to Reagan. More surprisingly, liberals began to conclude, If you can't beat him, join him. In combat with George W. Bush, they began finding ways to wrap themselves in Reagan's mantle at Bush's expense. In addition, many Americans, including many opinion leaders, genuinely revised their estimation of Reagan upward in the light of three consecutive presidents who seemed in varying ways to fall short of his model. Many intellectuals, in particular, altered their views when researchers published the drafts of Reagan's correspondence and radio addresses, work that demonstrated beyond reasonable doubt that Reagan was far from the "amiable dunce" described by critical commentators. Two of the last four academic surveys have rated Reagan among the top eight presidents in American history, and a third ranked him number eleven. Polls from 2006 and 2007 showed Reagan winning a plurality among Americans who were asked to identify the best president since World War II and the recent president they most wanted the next president to be like.

The depth of Americans' affection for Reagan can be measured by, among other things, the degree to which they have chosen to commemorate him in a variety of ways. The renaming of Washington DC's National Airport as Ronald Reagan Washington National Airport has been the highest-profile example, along with the naming of an aircraft carrier and an air force missile defense site. Since 1989, there have also been at least twenty-six streets and roads, fifteen schools, eight parks and community centers, four government buildings, a mountain in New Hampshire, and approximately forty other assorted locations and programs inside the United States named after the fortieth president. (There are also Reagan commemorations in a number of other countries, including Ireland, Hungary, Poland, and Grenada.)

The two most notable events illustrating Reagan's rise in status came in 2004, when a plethora of notable liberal Democrats took to the podium to praise Reagan at his death, and in 2007, when *Time* magazine devoted a cover story to the topic of how George W. Bush had fallen short of Reagan's greatness. In July 2004 Senator Edward Kennedy declared that Reagan had "revived the spirit of the Nation in that era, restored the power and vitality of the Presidency, and made it a vigorous and purposeful place of effective national and international leadership. . . . On foreign policy, he will be honored as the President who won the Cold War. . . . His deepest convictions were a matter of heart and mind and spirit, and on them, he was no actor at all." These conversions were doubtless based on some combination of sincere reflection, practical accommodation to Reagan's continuing popularity among Americans, and opportunistic hopes of using Reagan, jujitsu-style, as a weapon against Bush.

Reagan's postpresidential trajectory can be compared with Franklin Roosevelt's. Roosevelt—having brought the nation through the two supreme crises of depression and world war, and having died in office—was commemorated much more broadly and more quickly than Reagan. Roosevelt and Reagan each came under some assault both from their enemies, who claimed they were highly important but malignant, and their friends, who claimed they were benign but should have done more. Roosevelt's reputation among intellectuals, though better than Reagan's, has not been unmixed, as some blamed him for Yalta early on, and many have recently painted a picture of him as a political genius and an economic nincompoop. All the while he has remained popular with the American people.

One can pinpoint the moment when Roosevelt's memory was neutralized as a political boon for Democrats—the same moment, not incidentally, that his philosophical opponents embraced him. When Reagan, who had voted for FDR four times, quoted Roosevelt and the 1932 Democratic platform in his own 1980 nomination acceptance speech to argue for states' rights and balanced budgets, Republicans staked their own claim to the thirty-second president. FDR was hence simultaneously elevated to the status of a consensus hero and drained of ideological meaning. It may well be that Reagan himself has now entered a similar stage, in which Democrats concede to him his due, attempting to co-opt him and hence rendering him unusable by Republicans.

The exchange between Hillary Clinton and Barack Obama in early 2008, in which Clinton attacked Obama for saying something good about Reagan's leadership and Obama quickly backtracked, indicated that this process is far from complete (and may never be completed). Recently, there have also been signs of a renewed counteroffensive by liberals against Reagan, one key element of which has been an emphasis on Reagan the racially insensitive. This line of attack has focused on Reagan's 1980 campaign appearance at the county fair in Neshoba County, Mississippi, site of the 1964 murder of civil rights activists, where Reagan made a speech than included a reference to states' rights. Nevertheless, this effort is yet young, and it is too early to know whether Reagan's reputation among the general public will suffer because of it.

Testing Reputation against Reality

Reputation, of course, is one thing; reality is another. John F. Kennedy has high schools named after him all over America and consistently ranks high in public opinion polls about former presidents. Yet his short presidency witnessed few concrete accomplishments. What can be said of Ronald Reagan's legacy in terms of accomplishment?

One component of presidential greatness is whether a president had to rise to meet great challenges, such as the establishment of the federal government, civil strife, war abroad, or economic catastrophe at home. Reagan took office at a time of tangible economic and foreign policy crisis, an institutional crisis revolving around the viability of the presidency, a crisis of morale, and a quiet crisis of deteriorating social indices inherited from the 1960s and 1970s. The dominant economic paradigm of Keynesianism was failing and discredited by the simultaneous rise of inflation and unemployment. "Stagflation" and the "energy crisis" led economists ranging from Robert Heilbroner on the left to Alan Greenspan on the right to ask whether a free market economy could survive. Abroad, the Soviet empire was on the march, having engaged in an unprecedented military buildup and having acquired an average of one new country every six months from 1975 through the end of 1979. The Soviet invasion of Afghanistan, coupled with the revolution of the mad mullahs in Iran, introduced a new level of international danger. Soviet analysts declared that the "correlation of forces" was moving irreversibly in their favor, and analysts such as conservative Democrat Ben Wattenberg asked whether the West could survive. At the same time, indices of family breakdown, crime, drug use, and other social dysfunctions had worsened dramatically from 1960 to 1980.

President Jimmy Carter's pollster Patrick Caddell told Carter as he geared up for his reelection campaign that Americans were more pessimistic about the future than at any time since scientific polling began. Confidence in American institutions, particularly the presidency, had also collapsed among both the general public and scholars. This "crisis of confidence" was so severe that Carter made it the subject of one of the most important speeches of his presidency in July 1979. Of twentieth-century presidents, only FDR faced a combination of crises that were more threatening, and he was able to face them sequentially. Reagan had to face his crises simultaneously.

By 1989 America had vanquished the economic, foreign, and morale crises, and the social crisis had in many particulars stabilized or even begun receding. Indeed, the nation had greater success conquering stagflation during Reagan's two terms than it had conquering depression during Roosevelt's first two terms. Even if Reagan's presidency had no long-term effect on the nation except that he managed and overcame the crises he inherited—seeing the nation back to a path of noninflationary economic growth, restoring historic American confidence, and avoiding the global victory of the Soviet Union in the cold war at a moment of grave danger—Reagan's legacy would be substantial.

Another test of presidential greatness must be the magnitude of policy change wrought by the president in both the short and long terms. By these criteria, Reagan's legacy was also significant. While policy has oscillated over the last three decades, it is fair to say that the entire era has swung around a new baseline established by Reagan.

ECONOMIC POLICY

Reagan's economic policy was built on a theoretical repudiation of Keynesianism in favor of neoclassical free market economics drawing from strands including Milton Friedman's monetarism, the supply-side emphasis on microeconomic incentives, and Friedrich Hayek's antistatist plea against central planning. While no strand has come to dominate as Keynesianism used to, it is equally true that Keynesianism itself has never recovered its former position. Even former president Bill Clinton embraced balanced budgets, allegedly complaining early in his presidency that he had been reduced to an Eisenhower Republican. What remains of Keynesianism is the ad hoc application of modest, short-term fiscal stimuli in hard economic times, such as Clinton's aborted 1993 stimulus package, elements of the 2001 Bush tax cuts, and the stimulus plan adopted in early 2008. Clinton himself put the exclamation point on the death of Keynesianism as a coherent doctrine driving federal economic policy when, facing an imminent economic slowdown in 2000, he vetoed a congressional tax cut because it would have reduced the predicted budget surplus.

In terms of actual economic policy, the period since 1980 can be seen broadly as a Reagan era if one accepts a number of serious deviations as not exceeding the general bounds of such an era. Cuts in marginal income tax rates have remained a favorite policy of Republicans, and Democrats have not yet come close to undoing them completely, even when they have succeeded in raising taxes somewhat. Under Reagan, the Economic Recovery Tax Act of 1981 reduced the top individual income tax rate from 70 percent to 50 percent; the Tax Reform Act of 1986 further reduced the top rate to 28 percent. At its peak after the Clinton tax increase, the top rate did not exceed 39.6 percent, and it was again reduced in George W. Bush's tax cuts to 35 percent, half of what it was in 1980. At the bottom end, Reagan's 1986 tax reform eliminated 4 million working poor from the tax rolls, a trend that continued under both Clinton and Bush the younger. In between those in the top bracket, whose tax rate was sliced, and those at the bottom, who stopped paying income tax altogether, middle brackets were protected from inflationary "bracket creep" by the income tax indexation included in the Economic Recovery Tax Act, which the *New York Times* called "one of the fairest pieces of tax law in many a year." Since the mid-1980s, no one of either party has dared to tamper with indexation. Now, if politicians want a tax increase, they have to vote for it.

Perhaps the greatest failure of Reagan's tax legacy came not in the back-to-back tax increases of 1990 and 1993, which left these general outlines intact, but in the steady reversal of the 1986 tax simplification by presidents and Congresses of both parties. Although it was appealing in theory and almost certainly more efficient in practice, a tax system with fewer deductions and lower rates proved unsustainable in the face of political temptations. Even here, however, Reagan's influence continues to be felt: George W. Bush was poised to propose a major tax reform before being sidetracked by Iraq, Katrina, and the failure of his Social Security initiative. A variety of candidates in the 2008 presidential campaign likewise endorsed some form of income tax simplification, the most radical of which was Mike Huckabee's embrace of a national sales tax as a replacement for the income tax.

On spending, Reagan's legacy was more mixed. He succeeded in cutting discretionary domestic spending by one-third as a proportion of gross domestic product (GDP), and he clearly inspired the new Republican Congress of the mid-1990s to cut federal domestic spending again. When it came to entitlements, many of Reagan's efforts to rein in spending in the 1980s came to naught, most spectacularly with the disintegration of his own Social Security plan in the fall of 1981. Nevertheless, even entitlement spending had fallen slightly as a percentage of GDP by the end of the 1980s. Perhaps most important, Reagan contributed to the formation of a new policy environment that made the creation of major new entitlement programs impossible for over two decades and that has undone until now the appetite for the sort of class-based redistributionism that served as the basis of New Deal policy and politics. Not until late 2003 was a major new entitlement program launched—the Medicare prescription drug program, under the encouragement of George W. Bush—and it redistributed money not from the rich to the poor but from the young to the old. Until late in his presidency, Bush appeared utterly unconcerned with a new spurt in federal domestic spending. While his tax policy would have suited Reagan quite well, Bush's spending (in cooperation with a friendly Congress of a sort that Reagan never enjoyed) would not have been as welcome.

Other areas of economic policy have exhibited a similar pattern: some reaction against Reaganism after 1989 but general continued movement in his direction. Bill Clinton may have regulated more than Reagan did as measured by pages in the *Federal Register*, but his administration never approached the Carter administration's level of regulatory zeal, and there has been no significant effort to reregulate those industries that were deregulated in the late 1970s and 1980s. Free trade, which was a major element of Reagan's economic worldview, has been embraced by all of his successors thus far, though they sometimes found it prudent to trim (as did Reagan himself). Reagan advanced his views on monetary policy through his appointments to the Federal Reserve Board, and it is notable that Fed chairmen since the 1980s have been cut from the same cloth. After reappointing Paul Volcker in 1983, Reagan appointed Alan Greenspan in 1987; Greenspan was reappointed by George H. W. Bush, Bill Clinton (twice), and George W. Bush before being replaced by what Bush expected was the like-minded Ben Bernanke.

Altogether, Reagan strove to fashion an economic policy that limited government, maximized economic freedom, and encouraged decentralized, flexible entrepreneurship. In the broadest sense, Reagan's aim was to save and reinvigorate the free market system for reasons of both economic efficiency and political liberty. Although a number of specific policy decisions since 1980 have moved in the opposite direction, the aggregate result has been an economic structure that is much closer to Reagan's preferences than to, say, the preferences of Ted Kennedy, who also ran for president in 1980 and might have been elected president that year had circumstances been a bit different. In short, Reagan was important in inaugurating an era that has seen a quarter century of growth and prosperity broken only by rare and mild downturns. Since 1983, there have been only two relatively short and mild recessions. (At this writing, we may or may not be on the verge of a third recession.) By comparison, in the quarter century before 1983 there had been six recessions, some of them (including 1957–1958, 1974–1975, and 1981–1982) quite severe.

Of course, Reagan's economic legacy must include consideration of the unanticipated negative side effects, which form a familiar litany summarized as higher deficits and greater inequality. Yet on examination the side effects fall far short of outweighing the successes. Deficits were a result of Reagan's defense buildup and tax cuts—or, equally plausibly, of recession and entitlement spending traceable to earlier decades, whichever one prefers. Taking a long view, as a proportion of GDP, the

U.S. government brought in much more revenue and spent much less money on defense in the 1980s than it did in 1960, when there was a balanced budget. In that sense, the explosion of domestic spending since the early 1960s was the decisive difference. In any case, by 1989, the deficit was about where it had been in 1980, and it disappeared in the 1990s before reappearing after September 11, 2001. It is difficult to detect any long-term damage to the American economy produced by the deficits of the 1980s.

As for inequality, it is well documented that income inequality in America began rising around 1973 and has been rising more or less steadily ever since—that is to say, during the presidencies of Nixon, Ford, Carter, Reagan, Bush, Clinton, and Bush. Clearly, something more is at issue than Reagan's economic policies, even if one grants that those policies established the general direction of policy ever since. Liberal analysts such as Mickey Kaus conclude that Reagan's policies were responsible for no more than 20 to 25 percent of increased income inequality in the 1980s. If critics mean that Reagan emphasized property rights rather than so-called positive economic rights and that he consequently made untenable for almost three decades the use of government to launch new projects of class-based redistributionism, they are right. Reagan himself would undoubtedly have been pleased to take credit for the accomplishment.

FOREIGN POLICY

In foreign policy, Reagan likewise succeeded in dramatically changing U.S. policy. He revived containment and deterrence, building up American defenses and shoring up American allies from Germany to El Salvador. In this he differed from the Jimmy Carter of 1980 in degree and enthusiasm, not in kind; Carter had already moved in this direction after the Soviet invasion of Afghanistan. Reagan's more radical shift came in embracing an approach that put the United States on the strategic offensive in the cold war. Everything from the Strategic Defense Initiative to the "evil empire" speech to the invasion of Grenada to the Reagan doctrine of aiding anti-Communist guerrillas was part of that offensive, and the aim was nothing less than the defeat of the Soviet regime. By 1983, this drive had congealed into a policy defined by a series of secret national security decision directives. This was not a new idea—Barry

Goldwater wrote a book on this theme in 1962 with the title *Why Not Victory?*—but it was an idea that met enormous resistance in the intellectual world and in the foreign policy establishment. At the same time, Reagan was much more open than many of his conservative allies to negotiating the Soviet surrender with the right general secretary. More generally, Reagan found a middle way between Nixonian realpolitik and early Carteresque naiveté, embracing both a hard-headed understanding of power in the international arena and a principled understanding that regimes matter, and hence democracy matters.

Unlike his economic policies, Reagan's specific foreign policy innovations did not much outlast him—not because they failed but because they succeeded. When the Soviet Union disintegrated in December 1991, cold war strategy lost its direct relevance to policy debates. Nevertheless, as in the economic realm, the broad outlines of Reagan's foreign policy ideas have remained intact. The United States has remained engaged with the world, the advancement of democracy has remained an important goal of policymakers, and no president has eschewed the use of American power as Jimmy Carter did from 1977 to 1979 or as Democratic Congresses did from 1975 to 1979. George H. W. Bush may have tilted toward stability instead of human rights in China or the Balkans, but he was no Nixon, as Manuel Noriega discovered; Bill Clinton may have been distracted and even feckless, but he was no Carter or McGovern, as the Serbs could attest.

Reagan's foreign policy offered the development of a strategy that allowed the United States to strike hard against its enemies while minimizing its direct exposure to risk. Reagan understood that "regime change" was sometimes a legitimate option or even the best option, but he was usually committed to achieving it indirectly, by aiding indigenous forces to reclaim their own country. The United States largely followed this model in Afghanistan in 2001, when it allowed the Northern Alliance to spearhead the defeat of the Taliban. (Indeed, the Reagan doctrine could conceivably be updated for systematic use against state sponsors of terrorism and other rogue states.)

Renewed American engagement in the world since 1980 has been underpinned by a conceptual and rhetorical change wrought by Reagan. For most of the half decade before Reagan took office, the "Munich paradigm"—the direct appeal by policymakers to the lessons of World War II, particularly to the lesson that appeasement of tyrants makes the world a less safe place—had been superseded by the "Vietnam paradigm," which saw U.S. intervention in third world conflicts as the primary foreign policy mistake to be avoided. Reagan revived Munich as a key driving force of U.S. foreign policy and a key rhetorical device used to explain that policy, not just in the last stages of the cold war but by subsequent policymakers in Iraq and other crises. Reagan also undercut the Vietnam paradigm in another way, by refusing to allow the antiwar Left a monopoly on the definition of the lessons of the Vietnam War. In his 1980 campaign, Reagan famously called the Vietnam War a "noble cause," and throughout his presidency he made clear that he thought the lessons of Vietnam were to give American allies the support they needed to fight Communism on their own and, if it became necessary to use U.S. troops, to fight to win. Above all, for Reagan, the lessons of Indochina were written in the faces of the boat people and the million or more human beings liquidated by the Communists in Cambodia: we must not abandon to the tender mercies of our totalitarian foes those who are fighting for freedom. Traces of this argument, updated for use against Baathist and jihadist totalitarians, appeared again as recently as 2007, when George W. Bush argued that Americans must not abandon Iraqis as we abandoned our Vietnamese friends. To be sure, the Vietnam paradigm has never disappeared and has periodically been trotted out by opponents of American assertiveness abroad. But it has never dominated thinking—and has rarely won a policy debate—as it did in the period before Reagan's election.

Social Policy

Reagan was also deeply concerned with social trends, trends in constitutional understanding, and the effect both might have on the maintenance of the American republic. In this sense, his political notions were Tocquevillian, and he cited Tocqueville frequently in his public remarks.

Reagan's social policy combined an emphasis on individual responsibility for individual acts (hence a hard-nosed approach to crime and drugs) with an emphasis on community rather than governmental solutions to community problems (hence promotion of civil society). Both were undergirded by a solicitude for traditional family and religion that Reagan saw as the necessary guide and glue for free society. In other words, Reagan reconciled the supposed rift between economic or "libertarian" conservatives and social conservatives by contending that the concerns of social conservatives—strong families, traditional morality, a place for religion in the public square—were not only compatible with liberty but essential to its preservation. This argument, too, has subsequently been echoed by figures ranging from Joseph Lieberman in 2000 to Mitt Romney in 2007.

As president, Reagan's tools were limited, as are those of any president who wishes to effect social change. Law and policy were instruments, but rhetoric played perhaps a larger role here than elsewhere. Reagan faced high-profile setbacks in Congress, as constitutional amendments to restrict abortion and allow voluntary school prayer failed to receive the requisite two-thirds votes. Nevertheless, there was a real turnaround in social indices in the 1980s that has been sustained and broadened since then. Crime, violent crime, drug use, divorce, and abortion rates all stabilized or fell from 1980 to 1990. During the same period, volunteerism and charitable giving rose markedly, and there were unmistakable signs of some revival of religious sentiment and observation. Most of these social improvements were carried into the next decade and beyond. The degree to which Reagan and Reaganism contributed to this recovery of society from the self-inflicted blows of the 1960s and 1970s is impossible to untangle, but they were, at any rate, pieces of this recovery. What can be said is that Reagan established a new baseline of presidential leadership in respect to social concerns and that subsequent presidents (including Bill Clinton) have hewed close to that baseline. Reagan's spotlight on volunteerism was a theme shared by the first Bush, Clinton, and the second Bush; his support for tough sentencing, including the death penalty, likewise found consistent support; two of the subsequent three presidents were pro-life, and the other was compelled to say that he hoped abortion would be "rare" as well as safe and legal.

CONSTITUTIONAL CONCERNS

In terms of the Constitution, Reagan possessed and sought to advance a more complete and integrated constitutional vision than any president in the modern era. The defense of federalism was a central constitutional aim of the Reagan administration, but Reagan also aimed to revive traditional constitutional doctrine and practice in areas including separation of powers, enumeration of powers, and individual rights. Above all, he proposed not the repeal of the New Deal itself but the repeal of its underlying constitutional premise, which was that the federal government could permissibly do virtually anything that federal policymakers could imagine.

This innovation—it was so old that it seemed new—was promoted by Reagan through a four-part strategy of legislation, executive orders, judicial appointments, and rhetoric. The first took the form of successful legislation such as replacement of many categorical grants with block grants to state and local governments and budget changes that restricted federal revenues, cut state and local governments' dependence on federal funds, and tilted remaining aid to states and away from local governments. It also took the form of the unsuccessful New Federalism proposal outlined in Reagan's 1982 State of the Union address calling for a sorting out of social welfare programs to more clearly delineate the roles of each level of government. The second prong could be seen, for example, in Executive Order 12612, which required that federal agencies formally consider the impact on federalism of proposed policies. The third part consisted of a systematic effort to shape the federal judiciary and to point it in the direction of greater reliance on the original intent of the founders. Finally, Reagan simply talked about the Constitution more than any recent president, seeking to justify his views by reference to constitutional doctrine rather than simple practicality.

Here, one must seriously question the depth of Reagan's legacy in the years since 1989. To be sure, Reagan's constitutional vision has made incremental advances in areas such as affirmative action and forced busing, a somewhat stricter reading of the commerce clause, and federalism, not least when the landmark welfare reform of 1996 decentralized welfare policy and ended the federal welfare entitlement. The Republican takeover of Congress in 1994 seemed for a time to promise a sustained effort to restore the traditional Constitution. Reagan's judicial revolution spawned a broader movement of judicial conservatives, at least two of whom (John Roberts and Samuel Alito) wound up on the Supreme Court decades later. Even in the breach, Reagan's vision has sometimes been honored. In 1996, Bill Clinton vowed that "the era of big government is over" after having shunted aside a budget more reflective of principles of limited government than any in recent memory; in 2000, when both Al Gore and George W. Bush were promising big new intrusions of the federal government into education, both felt compelled to insist that they believed in local control of schools. And in one respect, at least, Reagan was highly successful: restoring a luster to the institution of the presidency that has not been lost despite the maladroitness or character deficits of his successors.

Nevertheless, in retrospect it seems clear that the constitutional component of Reaganism has fared less well than the economic and foreign policy components. Each prong of Reagan's strategy has suffered. While there have been legislative victories for federalism, for example in welfare reform, these have been offset by big gains for centralization in education and criminal justice. Executive orders like 12612 could be and were easily rescinded a few years later. Eight years of Clinton judicial appointments did much to counteract the impact of Reagan's eight years, though Bush the younger set the course back toward Reagan; even Reagan's own appointees, like Sandra Day O'Connor and Anthony Kennedy, often disappointed, at least by conservative standards. Rhetorically, even Republican presidents claiming Reagan as their inspiration have generally failed to articulate constitutional principles as part of their public argument. In their respective State of the Union addresses, Reagan referred to the Constitution almost three times as often as the first Bush and about five times as often as Clinton and the second Bush. Among Republicans, George W. Bush has particularly fallen down in any discussion of structural issues like federalism and limited government. This tendency has been consistent with his deliberate attempt to formulate a new "compassionate conservatism" less concerned with limited government.

On one hand, Reagan's failures in this area might be a reason to consider him less than a great president. Franklin Roosevelt, after all, had much greater (though not complete) success implanting his constitutional vision over the long term. On the other hand, perhaps it is not Reagan who failed but his successors, and perhaps their failure actually bolsters his own case for greatness. It should not be counted against him, but rather in his favor, that he is the only president since the New Deal to give consistent and significant consideration to the health and maintenance of the American constitutional order. Even Roosevelt's was a constitutionalism in reverse, a constitutional doctrine that defined itself by the absence of constitutionalism, by the evisceration of constitutional limits. If Tocqueville was right that centralization is the natural tendency of democracy while resistance to it is a matter of deliberate art, Reagan was a constitutional artist and a statesman; his immediate predecessors and successors were, for the most part, constitutionally passive, carried along by the tide when they were not rowing in its direction.

POLITICAL LEGACY

Electoral and political success is another possible component of presidential greatness. It is difficult to imagine any president seriously contesting for greatness who is unable to win reelection. At the other extreme, Franklin Roosevelt's four consecutive victories, in which he won a combined total of 88 percent of all electoral votes, are a significant factor in many scholars' conclusion that he ranks among the great. By way of comparison, Reagan won election against an incumbent president, won reelection in impressive fashion, and captured a total of 94 percent of all electoral votes in those two years—the highest percentage of any president in the extended twentieth century. (Of other two-term presidents, Eisenhower won 85 percent of electoral votes in his two elections, Nixon 76 percent, Clinton 70 percent, Wilson 68 percent, and George W. Bush 52 percent.) Reagan's 1984 reelection featured the largest electoral vote total (525) in American history, and his 1980 win featured the longest presidential coattails in congressional elections in any election after 1964.

Reagan's long-term policy legacy depended more than a little on his development of a long-term political coalition to support it. Reagan did more than anyone else to give the Republican Party a hold on the votes of southerners, religious conservatives of all denominations, and a respectable proportion of working-class whites while holding on to the traditional Republican base among middle-class professionals, businesspeople, and mainline Protestants. Reagan's coalition did not dominate as did Roosevelt's New Deal coalition, and he did not press his advantage in 1984 to win a mandate for big policy change. Nevertheless, his coalition evened the odds and became reliably competitive for the presidency and Congress.

Intertwined with Reagan's direct political success was the incidental political effect of his successful presidency. By the mere (or perhaps not so mere) fact of being elected and governing well, Reagan succeeded in making conservatism an acceptable, respectable, and safe option for millions of voters who had not previously seen it in that light. Before 1980 it was an open question whether an avowedly conservative nominee could win under any circumstances. Perhaps all were fated, like Goldwater, to fall before charges of extremism. Indeed, Jimmy Carter tried hard to duplicate Lyndon Johnson's 1964 campaign playbook, and for several weeks in the autumn of 1980, it remained possible that he might succeed. Reagan lanced that boil and in this way also fundamentally transformed the American political environment. This change was so thoroughgoing that most voters and most analysts simply take it for granted today. If one test of presidential greatness is whether a president can forge a new and more favorable political balance for himself and his party over the long run, Reagan passed—if not with an A+, perhaps with an A– or a B+.

RATING REAGAN

Altogether, by the objective standards that are most obvious, Reagan falls much closer to "great" than to "average." He did not achieve all that he or his supporters wanted, and there were serious shortcomings in his administration, but he faced, and faced down, historical crises for the United States; implemented a program that significantly changed the course of policy across a wide range of important areas, inaugurating a broad new policy era; won outsize electoral victories; and contributed mightily to the formation of a powerful political coalition and a new political environment that have lasted a generation.

By all but the most jaundiced accounts, Reagan possessed a largeness of spirit without which men must grasp in vain at presidential greatness. Reagan was also, as many called him, the Great Communicator. Often this appellation was fixed on him by adversaries for whom it was a backhanded compliment. The implication was clear: Reagan had style but no substance. However, for millions of Americans, Reagan was loved because he was uniquely successful at combining rhetorical substance and style. He sought to advance a substantive public philosophy that he had spent decades studying (and shaping), and he articulated that philosophy with uncommon verve. Reagan understood the importance of making a public argument, not only for winning immediate policy battles but for laying the groundwork for long-term policy and electoral victories. His success is more impressive in retrospect than it was at the time, for we have now seen just how difficult it is for politicians to match it. What for Reagan seemed effortless has proven beyond the reach of his successors of both parties.

Reagan used his rhetorical skills to lift Americans at a moment of significant danger at home and abroad. This accomplishment, like the skill that made it possible, is often dismissed as mere atmospherics. This is a mistake, for two reasons. First, it was a more important accomplishment than many understand. A healthy national spirit is important for sustaining internal well-being and essential for surviving in a dangerous world, especially for powers vested with great responsibilities. In its absence, nations wither, turn on themselves in recrimination, and become ever more vulnerable to the depredations of adversaries; in extreme cases of demoralization, they fail to perpetuate themselves or to defend themselves vigorously. Franklin Roosevelt is widely acclaimed as a great president because he stemmed the nation's downward psychological spiral and restored some hope in the nation's future, forestalling revolution and the democratic rise of radical demagogues; Winston Churchill is likewise acclaimed not for any specific military decisions he made but for the way he stiffened the resolve of the British nation at a moment when that resolve was all that stood between the West and utter defeat. One can easily imagine an alternative history in which the 1980s saw the further demoralization of the United States, with catastrophic economic, political, social, and, not least, international consequences. In the worst case, the collapse of American resolve might have invited Soviet victory in the cold war or a world war stumbled into by Soviet miscalculation.

Second, Reagan's ability to inspire was significant because of the way it was achieved. Far from representing mindless hoopla, Reagan raised American spirits and stiffened American resolve by conducting a vast exercise of reminding Americans about their own history, their own traditional principles, and their own national character. It was no coincidence that his farewell speech in January 1989 called on Americans to preserve their national memory. His version of American history did not necessarily correspond with versions most favored in the history departments of elite American universities, but so much the worse for them. To Reagan, faith in future progress could be justified only by reference to an American past that illuminated examples of progress and the political principles necessary to attain it. In so doing, Reagan repeatedly highlighted perhaps the most important political driving force of the American experience, the conviction that Americans are masters of their own fate and of the government they formed to achieve their ends. Reagan's message was empowering to ordinary Americans who felt that they had been run over roughshod by assorted deputies of the liberal welfare state, including unelected and unaccountable judges, unelected and unaccountable bureaucrats, and other miscellaneous experts and social engineers who had long been given the authority to rule by the doctrines of progressivism. To the "experts" Reagan said, Do not forget whom you serve. To distraught Americans he said, You are free people. Govern yourselves.

WAS REAGAN GOOD FOR AMERICA?

In the end, it is impossible to assess Reagan without venturing beyond objective standards into the realm of judgments about whether his presidency was actually good for the country. Here there can be no expectation of consensus. One can agree that Reagan was a successful policymaker, spokesman, and coalition builder, and that his successes were of considerable significance, without agreeing that the nation was better for them. Political scientist Walter Williams, for example, concedes that Reagan was the most consequential president since Roosevelt but holds him responsible for the plunge of America into plutocracy. Nevertheless, to leave this question begging is, ultimately, to fail. What president can be acclaimed great—or even considered for the honor—if his accomplishments were, in the final analysis, bad for America?

In the case of Ronald Reagan, my own view is that his accomplishments left the country better by a wide margin. Reagan should be considered a great or near-great president because his many accomplishments advanced great objects: the preservation of a polity in which individual liberty and limited, constitutional self-government would thrive; the preservation of a society in which liberty would coexist amiably with responsibility and morality; the preservation of Western civilization against the totalitarian barbarism of the twentieth century. Reagan's successes meant that the experiment in free society envisioned by the founders would not yet go quietly into the good night, as many in the 1970s feared, swept away by its enemies abroad or by the relentless tides of Tocqueville's democratic despotism, in which the nation "is reduced to nothing better than a flock of timid and industrious animals, of which the government is the shepherd."

The 1960s and 1970s brought some genuine benefits to American society, and these were not undone by the Reagan era. But they also brought a variety of political and social disasters to the nation. Reagan succeeded in imposing a much-needed balancing of the excesses of the preceding era of unlimited government and social permissiveness, and he constructed the political coalition that was necessary to sustain the balance for at least a generation.

Reagan also dreamed great dreams for his country, as many presidents do, but his dreams stood out for their uncommon and commendable humility. They were great dreams of a prosperous, creative, and noble society and a free world, but they did not revolve around the egotistical greatness of his own ambition or the pharaoh-like greatness of centralized power. The greatness of his dreams was contained entirely within the honor, decency, ambition, pluck, and common sense of the American people and the wisdom and ongoing relevance of the political principles that both defined and guided them. It is easy to pursue political dreams that carry with them the incidental by-product of enhancing one's own power; it is this sort of dream that the political class most easily understands and applauds. Indeed, it is this nexus—the intertwining of superficial benevolence and gross political self-interest—that has fed the growth of the welfare state since 1932. Commitment to self-abnegation, deliberately and systematically transferring power to others far from the center—state governments, entrepreneurs, consumers, local civic organizations—is rarely found and rarely appreciated in Washington. Reagan cut against this grain, and yet he prospered. In this sense, too, he could be considered great. Others who followed (the Republican Congress after 1998, for example) have shown just how difficult a politics of self-abnegation is, both to advance externally and to sustain internally.

In the final analysis, Reagan was almost certainly the most consequential president of the last half of the twentieth century. That he was an extraordinary president in many respects became clearer over time as his successors demonstrated just how hard an act he was to follow. There is also good reason to view his legacy as overwhelmingly benign.

Reagan's chief rival for greatness in the twentieth century, Franklin Roosevelt, faced larger crises, wrought a revolution in policy and public philosophy that was more extensive and harder to overturn, and formed a political coalition that was more dominant than Reagan's. On the other hand, Reagan's revolution was harder to achieve, facing as it did the entrenched guns of the mature welfare state; was more coherent; and actually enjoyed greater success in meeting its policy (as opposed to its partisan) objectives. Reagan was also almost certainly more thoughtful than Roosevelt and more informed about the economic conundrums that he was called on to alleviate. In contrast to Roosevelt, Reagan sought to promote individual responsibility and self-reliance, decentralization, and a Constitution that placed real boundaries around the ambitions of the federal government. At least some measure of greatness should be assigned on the basis of which approach is more likely in the long run to promote the freedom and well-being of the country.

A REAGAN DETOUR OR AN ENDURING REAGAN?

This leaves a final question. Were Reagan and Reaganism an aberration—as Richard Reeves once put it, "the Reagan detour"? Or will they continue to have enduring significance in American life? In one sense, a statute of limitations must exist on judging the ongoing influence of any political figure. Times change, memories fade, some innovations fail and are forgotten while others succeed and thereby render themselves irrelevant. As Reagan himself pointed out on many occasions, freedom is never more than one generation away from being lost, because each generation must face the world anew. No conceivable effort of Reagan (or of any president) to preserve liberty could be so profound that it could end not only all contemporaneous threats to liberty but all future ones as well.

Having said that, judgment of a president's legacy cannot avoid taking into account the enduring power of that legacy. Many perceive that the prospects in the near term are poor for the extension of the Reagan era. Indeed, commentators from E. J. Dionne to Patrick Buchanan have predicted that it is coming to a close, not least because George W. Bush unwittingly succeeded in destroying Reagan's electoral coalition. Others such as Bruce Bartlett have argued that Bush betrayed and jeopardized Reagan's policy legacy, a criticism that is clearly more plausible in some areas than in others. When it comes to taxes, attention to judicial nominations, social conservatism, and a foreign policy grounded in a philosophy of natural rights, Bush followed Reagan closely. When it comes to federal spending, especially discretionary domestic spending and the creation of the Medicare prescription drug program, Bush deviated sharply, as did his policies and pronouncements regarding limited government more generally. Whereas Reagan sought to abolish the federal Department of Education, Bush embraced the No Child Left Behind Act of 2001 and ballooned federal education spending. Whereas Reagan called on Americans to consult first principles before expanding government, Bush's first principle was "When people are hurting government has got to move." There is little of Reagan's constitutionalism, particularly his regard for federalism and enumerated powers, to be found in Bush's presidency. Future scholars may conclude that Bush, inadvertently to be sure, hollowed out conservatism and left it bereft of the high ground it once occupied on a number of issues. A Democrat in the White House is unlikely to revive Reagan's themes, at least in the short run. And while many Republicans lay claim to the Reagan mantle, more than a few commentators on the right as well as the left note how ritualistic, stale, and mechanical their claims are.

It is conceivable that the world has changed sufficiently from the world of 1980 that the framework that has most influenced American politics since then is no longer compelling to most Americans, in the same way that 1932 had lost its centrality by 1968 or certainly by 1980. Big government seems less threatening, undoubtedly because the successes of Reaganism have made it so. According to American National Election Studies, in 1980, a 49 percent to 15 percent plurality of American voters held that government was too powerful, a 34-point gap; by 2000 the figure was 39 percent to 17 percent, a gap one-third smaller than twenty years before. American engagement abroad faces challenges from powerful advocates of trade protectionism and of paralysis masquerading as multilateralism. Likewise, there may be a declining constituency for conservative social mores among the rising generation. All of this remains to be seen; even the Democratic victory in November was not enough to answer the questions with certainty. (Remember that 1992 was a false start that many interpreted incorrectly as the end of Reaganism.)

However, there are also reasons to expect that Reagan's influence will not be completely eclipsed anytime in the foreseeable future, though it may be challenged or even overtaken. Foremost among these is the fact that Reaganism was, as many of Reagan's critics complained, reactionary—not in the pejorative, ideological sense but in a simply descriptive sense. That is to say, Reagan's program represented the strength of the popular reaction against the steady growth of centralized government, erosion of traditional morality, and decline of American strength in the world wrought by modern liberalism.

It may be a different world from 1980, but it is not that different. It is not improbable that liberalism, unwilling or unable to constrain its own impulses, is fated to provide a continuous stream of provocations in both the social and economic realms. Indeed, progressive thinkers acknowledged a century ago that their conception of the role of government was not bounded by any intrinsic limits, only by practical calculations of the moment. Imagine that the Democratic sweep in 2008 will lead to a large tax increase or two, a new round of social engineering, and a few years of unrestrained regulating. Add a handful of liberal court appointments that produce new decisions imposing same-sex marriage and polygamy, a constitutional right to taxpayer funding of abortion, and a pledge of allegiance that is more acceptable to atheists and less acceptable to the other 90 percent of the population. Throw in an ignominious retreat from Iraq or some other foreign policy calamity, and one will more likely than not find Reaganism and the Reagan coalition alive and quite competitive. There remain significant numbers of Americans who are suspicious of centralized power, who retain a belief in the free enterprise system, and who are unwilling to throw overboard the moral conventions of Western civilization and the patriotic imperatives of national sovereignty, and it is not only possible but probable that liberals will succeed in mobilizing those Americans the very next time they are in a position to do so. The crucial question then will be whether leadership exists to take advantage of the moment. Such leadership cannot be taken for granted, but it can hardly be ruled out, either. Indeed, political success such as Reagan achieved will always serve as a magnet for imitation, however difficult such imitation may prove to be in practice.

Although Reagan's Republicans could chart a different course in 1981, they could not go back to 1928 as if Roosevelt and the intervening years had simply not happened. In the same way, even if Democrats can change the course of the nation going forward, it will never be 1979 again—nor do many Americans wish it could be. That is, perhaps, the simplest and best argument for the legacy of Ronald Reagan.

Is the "Age of Reagan" Over?

Steven F. Hayward

I think Ronald Reagan changed the trajectory of America in a way that, you know, Richard Nixon did not and in a way that Bill Clinton did not. He put us on a fundamentally different path because the country was ready for it. . . . I think it's fair to say that the Republicans were the party of ideas for a pretty long chunk of time there over the last ten, fifteen years, in the sense that they were challenging conventional wisdom.

—Barack Obama, January 14, 2008

The fact is that how we talk about the Reagan era still matters immensely for American politics.

—Paul Krugman, *New York Times*, January 21, 2008

Although some liberals, such as Barack Obama and Paul Krugman, have praised Ronald Reagan, most conservatives now despair that no one measures up to his standards. All of this calls to mind what Richard Hofstadter wrote about Franklin Roosevelt: "No personality has ever expressed the American popular temper so articulately or with such exclusiveness. . . . In the age of the New Deal it was monopolized by one man, whose passing left liberalism demoralized and all but helpless." Substitute "Reagan" for "Roosevelt" and "conservatism" for "liberalism," and Hofstadter's quote might apply to the passing of Reagan. If so, then both Roosevelt and Reagan stand out as enduring forces in American politics. But with regard to Reagan, liberals and conservatives offer differing perspectives.

A LIBERAL IN CONSERVATIVE CLOTHING?

Some liberals have embraced Reagan as a liberal in conservative clothing. Perhaps the best early example of this is *Washington Monthly* writer Joshua Green, who wrote in January 2003 that "many of [Reagan's] actions as president wound up facilitating liberal objectives. What this clamor of adulation is seeking to deny is that beyond his conservative legacy, Ronald Reagan has bequeathed a liberal one."[1] Green's article featured a cartoon rendering of Reagan assuming the mantle of FDR, complete with upturned cigarette holder.

More recently, John Patrick Diggins argued in his book *Ronald Reagan: Fate, Freedom, and the Making of History,* "Far from being a conservative, Reagan was the great liberating spirit of modern American history, a political romantic impatient with the status quo. . . . Reagan's relation to liberalism may illuminate modern America more than his relation to conservatism. What Reagan sought to do for America has been the goal of liberalism since the eighteenth-century Enlightenment: to get rid of authority, the meddlesome intrusions of controlling institutions, whether of church or state." Diggins's thesis is correct in the sense that we are all "liberals" in the eighteenth-century meaning of the term. To this extent, Reagan was trying to revive or reform the one embattled or attenuated branch of liberalism to which the Right finds allegiance. Moreover, toward the end of his preface, Diggins discloses that part of his purpose is "to rescue Reagan from many of today's so-called Reaganites."[2]

The liberal suggestion that Reagan was a closet or confused liberal deserves to be treated seriously, because it allows me to challenge my own premise: was there an Age of Reagan to begin with?

A CONSERVATIVE BETRAYAL

A large number of conservatives made the case for disappointment, verging on betrayal, both during Reagan's presidency and immediately after he left office. For example, the Winter 1984 issue of the Heritage Foundation's flagship journal, *Policy Review,* contained the symposium "What Conservatives Think of Reagan." Now recall that in the winter of 1984 the Democrats were engaged in a spirited nomination battle to see who could best reestablish old-school liberalism and overthrow the Reagan usurpation. As late as December 1983, some polls found

Reagan trailing the putative strongest Democratic challenger, Senator John Glenn, and it was far from clear that the economic expansion that showed signs of robustness in 1983 would continue. In the midst of this uncertain political map, conservatives such as Senator William Armstrong said, "What's the sense of having a Republican administration and a Republican Senate if the best we can do is a $200 billion deficit?" Terry Dolan, the head of the National Conservative Political Action Committee, which had played a significant role in the 1980 election, complained, "There has been no spending cut. There has been no turnover of control to the states. There has been no effort to dismantle the Washington bureaucratic elitist establishment. . . . The question when Reagan got elected was whether he was going to be closer to Eisenhower as a caretaker or to Roosevelt as a revolutionary. He's been generally closer to Eisenhower, preserving the status quo established by previous liberal administrations." On and on the conservative commentariat piled on. Conservative journalist M. Stanton Evans: "This has been essentially another Ford administration. It has been business as usual, not much different from any other Republican administration in our lifetime." Howard Phillips: "This has been more like Ford's presidency than a real revolution." Paul Weyrich: "The radical surgery that was required in Washington was not performed."

Much the same kind of thing was said about Reagan at the end of his second term. Midge Decter wrote in *Commentary* in 1991, "There was no Reagan Revolution, not even a skeleton of one to hang in George Bush's closet." "In the end," concurred William Niskanen, chairman of Reagan's Council of Economic Advisers, "there was no Reagan Revolution." It was Niskanen, by the way, who criticized the Tax Reform Act of 1986, which raised corporate income taxes in order to lower top individual income tax rates all the way to 28 percent, telling Reagan in a meeting, "Walter Mondale would have been proud."

These conservative complaints about Reagan were extended to foreign policy as well. As early as 1982, many conservatives were dismayed at Reagan's lifting of the grain embargo against the Soviet Union and at what they saw as a tepid response to the imposition of martial law in Poland and the crushing of Solidarity. George Will complained that the Reagan administration "loved commerce more than it loathed Communism." Norman Podhoretz wrote, "Where Poland was concerned, the Administration seemed more worried about hurting a few bankers than about hurting the Soviet empire."[3] *National Review* called the sanctions "marginal deprivations." The Committee for the Free World placed a full-page ad in the *New York Times* calling for a tougher response. *Human Events'* front-page article was savage: "It may seem rather harsh to say so, but the Reagan Administration is beginning to acquire the reputation of one that sounds a bit like Churchill but frequently acts like Chamberlain."[4] More damning than the criticism from Reagan's ideological allies was the praise he received from liberals, who normally disdained Reagan's every breath. *New York Times* columnist Anthony Lewis wrote a column approving Reagan's mild sanctions against Poland titled "Reagan Gets It Right," and Jimmy Carter signaled his approval: "He's comin' toward me all the time."

These complaints became more vociferous in the second term, as Reagan began his summits with Gorbachev and began reaching arms agreements. "Some conservatives worry that Reagan has been beguiled by Gorbachev to the detriment of American interests," Hedrick Smith reported in the *New York Times Magazine* in 1988. Republican senator James McClure of Idaho worried, "We've had leaders who got into a personal relationship and have gotten soft—I'm thinking of Roosevelt and Stalin."[5] If McClure's comment was less than subtle, other conservatives didn't even try to be artful. Conservative activist Howard Phillips said Reagan was "fronting as a useful idiot for Soviet propaganda." There was talk among some conservatives of founding an "anti-appeasement alliance" to oppose Reagan's diplomatic overtures to the Soviet Union. These doubts about Reagan were not limited to the know-nothing ranks of right-wingers. George Will, Reagan's great friend and frequent booster, charged that Reagan was engaging in "the moral disarmament of the West by elevating wishful thinking to the status of political philosophy."[6]

With the subsequent revelations of what was actually known and taking place behind the scenes, we have a very different view of the matter today. About Reagan's cold war statecraft, George Will today freely admits, "I was wrong." But the sour evaluation on the domestic side of the ledger remains today much as it was twenty years ago. As William Voegeli surveyed the scene recently in the *Claremont Review of Books,*

> In 1981, the federal government spent $678 billion; in 2006, it spent $2,655 billion. Adjust that 292% increase for inflation, and the federal government is still spending 84% more than it

did when Reagan became president—in a country whose population has grown by only 30%.

To put the point another way, if per capita spending after 1980 had grown at the rate of inflation, federal outlays would have been $1,883 billion in 2006 instead of $2,655 billion. The 41% increase from 1981 to 2006 *is* considerably lower than the 94% increase in real, per capita spending in the previous 25 years from 1956 to 1981. In the last two decades, the federal establishment grew steadily, rather than dramatically. Nonetheless, Reagan's pledge to curb the government's size and influence has hardly been fulfilled. Inflation-adjusted federal spending increased in every year but two over the past 26 years.[7]

The late Thomas B. Silver argued, "Judged by the highest goal he set for himself, [Reagan] was not successful. That goal was nothing less than a realignment of the American political order, in which the primacy of the New Deal was to be challenged and overthrown. It cannot be said that Reagan in any fundamental way dismantled or even scaled back the administrative state created by FDR."[8]

THREE OBSERVATIONS

Three observations or themes should be brought to bear on this conservative discontent. First, it is possible to adduce some counterarguments to this brief, such as noting that Reagan almost surely lowered the growth rate of government spending substantially below what it would have been in a second term of Jimmy Carter or even under some other less ideological Republican president such as Howard Baker or George H. W. Bush. And the failure thesis could be said to have sold short a number of important accomplishments in reforming regulation and legal policy in several areas such as energy, antitrust, trade, civil rights, and financial markets. The aforementioned William Voegeli offers the counterargument even in the realm of broad fiscal policy: "One yardstick may help conservatives feel a little better about themselves. In 1981 federal spending was 22.2% of GDP; last year [2006] it was 20.3%. This measure hovered in a very narrow band for the whole era, never exceeding 23.5% or falling below 18.4%. Adding expenditures by states and localities confirms the picture of a rugby match between liberals and conservatives that is one interminable scrum in the middle of the field. Spending by all levels of government in America amounted to 31.6% of GDP in 1981, and 31.8% in 2006."

While this kind of stock-taking of the policy balance sheet is important and necessary, it is a weak argument. The suggested bumper sticker slogan—"Reagan: He Kept Things from Getting Even Worse"—is hardly one to stir the masses. Moreover, the gap between the professed goal of the Reagan revolution—"to curb the size and influence of the federal establishment and to demand recognition of the distinction between the powers granted to the federal government and those reserved to the states or to the people," as Reagan put it in his first inaugural address[9]—and what was actually achieved prompts the most searching questions about the durability of liberal governance. It turns out that merely winning a landslide election for the presidency or, as we learned in the 1990s, winning control of Congress in a revolutionary mood is not sufficient for a thorough conservative revolution in governance. The problem is deeper than anyone imagined in 1980. In reality it is a constitutional problem.

The second observation is that much of the conservative discontent derives from the categorical imperatives of ideological fervency, which are the lifeblood of party politics and political activism but often distract from perceiving real changes and achievements. It is striking to compare Reagan with Franklin Roosevelt, the liberal icon, for both suffered from the contemporaneous disappointment of their ideological supporters. Like Reagan and the conservatives, during FDR's time liberals were often frustrated with him and thought the New Deal fell far short of what it should accomplish. The *New Republic* lamented in 1940 "the slackening of pace in the New Deal" and also noted that "the New Deal has been disappointing in its second phase." The philosopher John Dewey and Minnesota's Democratic governor Floyd Olson, among others, complained that the New Deal hadn't gone far enough to abolish the profit motive as the fundamental organizing principle of the economy, and Socialist Party standard-bearer Norman Thomas scorned FDR's "pale pink pills." Historian Walter Millis wrote in 1938 that the New Deal "has been reduced to a movement with no program, with no effective political organization, with no vast popular party strength behind it, and with no candidate."[10] There's just no pleasing some people.

This leads to my third observation, which concerns having a clearer recognition of a central aspect of party politics that was poorly perceived or actively misrepresented, especially by the media in the 1980s, and that is still not adequately recognized by historians today. Here again a comparison of Reagan and FDR is helpful. Both men had to battle not only the other party but also their own. Each man by degrees successfully transformed his own party while frustrating and deflecting the course of the rival party. This, I suggest, is the heart of the real and enduring Reagan revolution or Age of Reagan.

Liberal ideologues who despaired over the limits of the New Deal overlooked that FDR had to carry along a large number of Democrats who opposed the New Deal. Reagan's experience was similar to FDR's, as he had to carry along a number of Republicans who were opposed to or lukewarm about his conservative philosophy. This problem would dog Reagan for his entire presidency. Robert Novak observed in late 1987, "True believers in Reagan's efforts to radically transform how America is governed were outnumbered by orthodox Republicans who would have been more at home serving Jerry Ford."[11] In other words, FDR and Reagan both had to conduct two-front political struggles: against the main ranks of the other party and against the reactionary establishment within their own parties. As Harvey Mansfield put it in 1983, "The debate in American politics today, one can say with little exaggeration, is within the Republican party between those with ideas and the prudent distrusters of ideas."[12]

Had it been within the power of the "prudent distrusters" of the GOP establishment in 1980, the party's presidential nomination would surely have gone to Gerald Ford, George H. W. Bush, Howard Baker, Bob Dole, or John Connally before Reagan. By 1980 many Republicans in Washington could be considered victims of the political equivalent of the Stockholm syndrome, according to which hostages come to sympathize with their captors. Having been in the minority for so long, many Washington Republicans had come to absorb the premises of establishment liberalism, preferring to offer a low-budget version of the Democratic platform.

REAGAN'S CHALLENGE TO THE ESTABLISHMENT

Reagan's dramatic landslide election in 1980, and the mandate it conferred, might be said to pose two problems: Democrats had to figure out how to oppose Reagan; Republicans, how to contain him. Even though Republican senators owed their newfound and much coveted committee chairmanships to Reagan's coattails, old establishment bulls like Bob Dole, Howard Baker, Pete Domenici, Charles Percy, Charles Mathias, John Warner, Robert Packwood, Slade Gorton, Larry Pressler, Lowell Weicker, Robert Stafford, John Chaffee, and Mark Hatfield were distinctly unenthusiastic about Reagan and laid repeated roadblocks in Reagan's path. Dole and Domenici were key senators on the finance committee, through which much of Reagan's economic policy would have to pass. Hatfield, the new chairman of the appropriations committee, didn't care much for Reagan's proposals to cut social spending, eliminate cabinet departments, or privatize the Bonneville Power Administration ("Over my dead body," Hatfield roared). His fellow Oregonian Packwood, chairman of the National Republican Senatorial Committee, attacked Reagan as an obstacle to a Republican realignment. Charles Percy, chairman of the foreign relations committee, openly criticized Reagan's arms control diplomacy and often put holds on Reagan's diplomatic appointees. Percy found ample Republican support from Pressler and Mathias. Several of these senators had contested for the GOP nomination in 1980 and were unchastened by their rout, chiefly because each thought himself better qualified than Reagan to sit in the Oval Office. Reagan once upbraided Howard Baker, "Remember, Howard, I'm president and you're not."

Much of the time these GOP senators acted as though they were in opposition; they shared little or none of Reagan's ideological or partisan spiritedness, giving proof to Eugene McCarthy's quip that the principal function of liberal Republicans "is to shoot the wounded after the battle is over." Reagan noted this problem from time to time and expressed privately a high degree of contempt for Capitol Hill Republicans. In fact, although I have not tallied up the references in Reagan's published diaries, reading through them, one gets the impression that Reagan complained at least as much about timid Republicans on Capitol Hill as about Tip O'Neill and other Democrats. In a diary entry in 1984, complaining about Hatfield's opposition to an administration position on the budget, Reagan ruefully commented, "With some of our friends we don't need enemies." In another diary entry, Reagan referred to Lowell Weicker as "a pompous, no good fathead," and on another occasion, he complained that "Weicker had the gall to question me—I think I did him in." More than once after a disappointing show of support from congressional Republicans, Reagan wrote in his diary, "We had rabbits when we needed tigers." The party split in the Senate existed also in the House, though the more populist and freewheeling nature of the House gave the insurgent conservatives more latitude to assert themselves.

The lesson of FDR and Reagan is that changing one's own party can be more difficult than beating the opposition party in elections. Woodrow Wilson wrote, "If the president leads the way, his party can hardly resist him." Perhaps, but the longer tenure in Washington of most House and Senate members, combined with the prerogatives of the separation of powers, feeds their intransigence. FDR grew impatient as his own party blocked his legislative agenda during his second term, and thus he attempted to purge the Democratic Party of anti–New Dealers in the 1938 election cycle. This gambit failed worse than his court-packing scheme and resulted in a Republican rout at the polls. (Democrats lost seventy-one House seats and five Senate seats in 1938.)

Reagan, whether by temperament or conviction or both, rejected any notion of leading a Republican purge. To the contrary, he replicated his two-front struggle against liberalism and establishment Republicanism within his own senior staff at the White House, resulting in the well-advertised split between the so-called ideologues and pragmatists. Lawrence Eagleburger, who served in Reagan's State Department and later briefly served as secretary of state under President George H. W. Bush, observed early in Reagan's first term that his administration resembled "a coalition government" more akin to what might be seen in a multiparty parliamentary government in Europe. Movement conservatives bristled at seeing the GOP establishment so well represented in Reagan's inner circle, and to be sure, the "pragmatists" were more adroit at infighting and using press leaks in attempts to alter Reagan's course.

At the same time, neither movement conservatives nor the media perceived how well this arrangement served Reagan or, indeed, how it matched his experience in California, where Reagan blended moderate Republicans from the campaign of his vanquished primary foe, George Christopher, with movement conservatives. Reagan tried to explain it in this exchange from a 1981 press conference:

Question: Can I ask you one more question? There have been specific reports that your Secretary of State and Secretary of Defense are not getting along and that they argue in front of you. Can you comment on those reports?

President Reagan: The whole Cabinet argues in front of me. That was the system that I wanted installed.[13]

WASHINGTON, LINCOLN, ROOSEVELT, AND REAGAN

In a manner that eludes many historians, political scientists, and reporters, the most successful presidencies tend to be those that have factional disagreements within their inner councils, whereas sycophantic administrations tend to get in the most trouble. Fractiousness in an administration is a sign of health: the Jefferson-Hamilton feud in Washington's administration, the rivalry within Lincoln's cabinet, and the odd combination of fervent New Dealers and conventional Democrats in FDR's White House provided dynamic tension that contributed to successful governance. Though the partisans of the distinct camps in the Reagan White House would be loathe to admit it, their feuding probably contributed to better policy in many cases. An attempted Reaganite purge, of either the party or his own staff, might well have backfired and snuffed out the spontaneous slow-motion revolution within the party that was already under way and that gained new momentum in the 1990s under the spur of figures such as Newt Gingrich. Gingrich was frequently among conservatives who expressed frustration with Reagan. "Ronald Reagan is the only coherent revolutionary in an administration of accommodationist advisers," Gingrich complained in 1984. "The problem was that Reagan's people were so excited by victory, they forgot they didn't control the country. They didn't control the House and they didn't really control the Senate. They didn't in fact have real power, but psychologically they acted as if they did."[14]

At one White House meeting late in Reagan's second term, after Gingrich laid out complaints about important things the administration had left undone, Reagan put his arm around Gingrich and said in his typically gentle fashion, "Well, some things you're just going to have to do after I'm gone." To be sure, the so-called pragmatist-ideologue split in the White House was reflected in the widely varying characters of agencies and cabinet departments. Where there was a concentration of movement conservatives, such as at the Justice Department, the

Federal Trade Commission, and the Office of Management and Budget, there were substantial efforts to make fundamental policy changes and to tame the permanent bureaucracy. In departments and agencies that lacked a critical mass of ideologues, such as the Department of Education during Reagan's first term and the Department of Labor, there was little or no conservative reform.

THE ULTIMATE TRIUMPH

Twenty years later, nearly every Republican claims to be a Reagan Republican, as he has become the standard against which to measure Republicanism, just as FDR became the standard for two generations of Democrats. Many of the so-called pragmatists of the Reagan years are now in the political wilderness and admit to having been had by the wily Reagan. This enduring realignment within the Republican Party also represents the triumph of a practical principle the Reaganites understood clearly but were unable to implement with complete success: personnel is policy. *National Review* publisher William Rusher wrote in 1984, "[Reagan] has put conservatives into lower echelons of government. This means that in the next conservative administration, conservatives can go to the higher echelons." Rusher added, "Reagan has been criticized for drawing his top people from outside the conservative ranks. But previously, there was not a soul in the conservative movement who had been postmaster of Dogpatch, Kentucky. How can you have a reasonable agenda for redesigning the Environmental Protection Agency when no conservative has ever served there? Reagan has been like Columbus. He has led us ashore on a continent many of us have never seen or been on." And so one of the notable aspects of the George W. Bush years was the many junior Reaganites who emerged as key people for George W. Bush to advance to senior positions, such as Paul Wolfowitz, John Bolton, Paula Dobrianski, and most especially John Roberts and Samuel Alito.

"ORIGINAL INTENT": REAGAN'S MOST ENDURING LEGACY

The ascension of Roberts and Alito, along with a number of lower court appointments of distinguished conservative jurists, raises perhaps the most salient aspect of the Reagan legacy. Gradually I have come to the view that the most important Reagan initiative on the domestic scene was not tax cuts or supply-side economics but Attorney General Ed Meese's decision in 1985 to make a sustained and prominent public controversy over the idea of "original intent." We underestimate the importance of this because of the mixed results we see in the practice of the judicial branch of our government on all levels. But in launching this controversy in such a high-profile manner, Meese reopened a fundamental quarrel that liberals had thought was more or less closed and over with. No prominent Republican had seriously advanced such an argument since Coolidge. The public fight Meese started over original intent, legal scholar Jonathan O'Neill wrote, "constituted the most direct constitutional debate between the executive branch and the Court since the New Deal."[15] Meese and his Justice Department compatriots were attempting nothing less than to wrest the Constitution away from a self-appointed legal elite and return it to the people.

The furious reaction from liberals assured that Meese's initiative would not dissipate into the mists, and it is still with us today. And notwithstanding the catastrophic defeat of Robert Bork's nomination to the Supreme Court in 1987, I offer the summary argument that the proponents of "originalism" have the initiative in the arena of jurisprudence today. Time and space limitations prevent me from developing this analysis fully here, but suffice it to note the number of liberal legal scholars who strain to recast their judicial activism in some kind of originalist garb, such as Akhil Amar's inventive doctrine of "intertextualism" and Bruce Ackerman's constitutional "dualism."[16] Having explicitly rejected the American founding as obsolete or irrelevant to modern conditions in the Progressive Era one hundred years ago, liberals are now finding themselves compelled to reground their views somehow in the principles of the founding era. That they do so with ahistorical or mischievous constructions of the founding should not distract us from the partial victory this represents for conservatism: rhetorical concessions typically precede substantive concessions. And one can point to a number of court decisions over the last fifteen years in which the spirit of originalism has made itself evident.

To be sure, this revolution is halting and tentative and might yet be reversed with a few bad appointments to the high court in the coming years. Yet it points to the most enduring legacy of what I have called the Age of Reagan. It was put best by Midge Decter, who complained, as I noted above, that "there was no Reagan Revolution." She added, "But what he did leave behind was something in the long run probably more important—a series of noisy open debates about nothing less than the meaning of decency, the limits of government, the salience of race, the nature of criminal behavior."

A Detour or a Main Road

I think Decter's observation about the "noisy open debates" Reagan started is confirmed by another of Reagan's surprising recent liberal admirers, Richard Reeves. In 1985 Reeves published *The Reagan Detour*, in which he suggested that liberals should relax. The Reagan presidency, he wrote, would turn out to be a brief interlude in the inexorable march of liberalism: "Ideas and issues . . . will inevitably bring liberalism and the Democrats back into fashion and power—sooner rather than later." When Reagan left office in 1989, Reeves wrote in his syndicated column, "It will be quite a while before history judges these eight years," but Reeves was ready to judge them right away. "I am a detractor. . . . Reagan gave it his best shot, but he failed." Throughout the George H. W. Bush years, Reeves filed column after column embellishing the liberal campfire ghost stories that Reagan favored the rich, reduced the middle class, and saddled our children with endless debt.

With the coming of Bill Clinton, Reeves thought he had found vindication. "It is a pleasure to watch this president work," Reeves wrote in early 1994. "Whatever else he has done in his first year, Clinton has shown he has both ideas and testosterone—and maybe he thinks that will be enough to move the nation off the Reagan detour and back into more caring directions." Shortly before the 1994 election, I suggested to Reeves in a debate in Santa Barbara that if the imminent election went as the polls suggested it would, he might need to reissue *The Reagan Detour* under a new title, *The Reagan Main Road*.

At first Reeves shared in the liberal denial, writing that the 1994 election was a populist revolt by white men who wanted to be back in control again. But then something seemed to snap. Starting in 1996, Reeves began to upgrade Reagan's status: "I was no fan of Ronald Reagan, but I think I know a leader when I see one, even if I do not want to follow where he is leading. . . . He was a man of conservative principle and he damned near destroyed American liberalism. Reagan was larger than he seemed, indeed larger than life, even if our historians do not quite get it yet." A year later Reeves wrote of Clinton, "Wittingly or not, the Democrat who ran as the agent of change gave up after a couple of years and joined the Reagan revolution." By 1999 Reeves's capitulation was complete: "Reagan, in fact, is still running the country. President Clinton is governing in his shadow, trying, not without some real success, to create a liberal garden under the conservative oak. In the next wave of history, when Americans have forgotten some of his failings, Reagan will probably be classed as a 'near-great' president."

And so Reeves belatedly took up the challenge of capturing Ronald Reagan's entire presidency in order to complete a triptych along with his previous presidential studies of John F. Kennedy and Richard Nixon. The result is *President Reagan: The Triumph of Imagination.* Twenty years ago bookmakers would have given very long odds against ever seeing a liberal grandee like Richard Reeves using the words "Reagan" and "triumph" in the same sentence, let alone in the title of a book. Reeves has come nearly full circle; far from being a mere hiatus in liberalism's long march, Reagan "made [the GOP] the dominant party in the country by turning the political populism of Franklin D. Roosevelt on its ear; the enemy of the working man is no longer big business but big government."

NOTES

1. Joshua Green, "Reagan's Liberal Legacy," *Washington Monthly,* January–February 2003.

2. John Patrick Diggins, *Ronald Reagan: Fate, Freedom, and the Making of History* (New York: Norton, 2007), xvii, 4, xxii.

3. "After I wrote that article," Podhoretz later recalled, "Reagan called me and spent half an hour on the phone reassuring me he was serious about the Soviets. What he basically said was: Trust me, they're in more economic trouble than people realize, and I'm going to put the squeeze on them."

4. "Is Reagan Foreign Policy Different from Carter's?" *Human Events,* December 26, 1981, 1.

5. McClure quoted in Hedrick Smith, "The Right against Reagan," *New York Times Magazine,* January 17, 1988, 38.

6. Will quoted in Dinesh D'Souza, *Ronald Reagan: How an Ordinary Man Became an Extraordinary Leader* (New York: Free Press, 1997), 185.

7. William Voegeli, "The Trouble with Limited Government," *Claremont*

Review of Books, Fall 2007, http://www.claremont.org/publications/crb/id.1495/article_detail.asp.

8. Thomas B. Silver, "Reagan's Failure" (unpublished manuscript in the author's possession).

9. Ronald Reagan, inaugural address (Washington, DC, January 20, 1981), Public Papers of President Ronald W. Reagan, Ronald Reagan Presidential Library, http://www.reagan.utexas.edu/archives/speeches/publicpapers.html.

10. Millis quoted in James MacGregor Burns, *Roosevelt: The Lion and the Fox* (New York: Harcourt, Brace, 1956), 375.

11. *National Review,* November 20, 1987, 49.

12. Harvey C. Mansfield Jr., "The 1982 Congressional Election: Reagan's Recalcitrant Economy," in *America's Constitutional Soul* (Baltimore: Johns Hopkins University Press, 1991), 44. This chapter was originally published as "The American Congressional Election," *Government and Opposition* 18 (1983): 144–56.

13. In a 1983 interview with *USA Today,* Reagan dilated the point: "I understand that in the past, Cabinets, for example—each person had his own turf and no one else in the Cabinet would talk about a decision affecting the turf of that one Cabinet member. I don't do business that way. Ours is more like a board of directors. I want all the input, because there are very few issues that don't lap over into other areas. . . . The only thing different from a board of directors is that I don't take a vote. I know that I have to make the decision."

14. Newt Gingrich, "What Conservatives Think of Ronald Reagan," *Policy Review,* Winter 1984, 16.

15. Jonathan O'Neill, *Originalism in American Law and Politics: A Constitutional History* (Baltimore: Johns Hopkins University Press, 2005), 157.

16. See Daniel A. Farber and Suzanna Sherry, *Desperately Seeking Certainty: The Misguided Quest for Constitutional Foundations* (Chicago: University of Chicago Press, 2002), esp. 75–96.

REAGAN'S OPEN-FIELD POLITICS

Michael Barone

In 2008—forty years after Ronald Reagan briefly campaigned for the 1968 Republican presidential nomination, thirty-two years after he almost wrested the 1976 presidential nomination from Gerald Ford, twenty-eight years after he won the presidency at age sixty-nine in 1980, and nineteen years after he left the White House in 1989—it said something about the importance of Reagan's legacy that it was still considered relevant forty years after he entered presidential politics.

Throughout the 2008 presidential campaign, many conservatives cried out for another Reagan to lead the Republican Party, and every Republican candidate for the presidential nomination claimed to be a Reagan Republican. Critics simultaneously praised candidates as Reagan Republicans and criticized them for allegedly abandoning Reagan's principles. In the contest for the Democratic nomination, in contrast, there was scarcely any mention of Reagan at all. Democratic candidates aimed most of their criticisms at George W. Bush and carefully refrained from attacking a man who is regarded by most Americans as a good president and, by many, a great president.

FRANKLIN ROOSEVELT AND RONALD REAGAN

My own view is that we have emerged from a period in which our politics has been polarized largely along the lines set by Ronald Reagan and that we are in, as we were in the years when Reagan was running for president, a new era. And I think there is an analogy here between the Republican Reagan and the Democratic president for whom he voted four times, Franklin Roosevelt. Both were presidents in difficult times and both achieved some but not all of their policy and political goals. Both left office just before the United States won major victories, over the Axis powers in World War II and over Soviet Communism in the cold war. Both left legacies to their parties that shaped their approaches to public policy and gave them wide appeal to the public. In 1958, thirteen years after Roosevelt's death, American voters elected a Congress with more New Dealers than any Congress during Roosevelt's years in office. That New Dealer majority had effective control over public policy for close to a decade, with some exceptions. In 1994, five years after Reagan's retirement from office, American voters elected a Congress with more Reagan Republicans than any Congress during Reagan's presidency. That Reaganite majority had effective control over public policy for close to a decade, with some exceptions.

The elections of the late 1960s and early 1970s deprived liberal Democrats of their effective control of Congress. More important, the times changed. New problems were faced, new issues were raised, and new challenges appeared. The Democratic Party largely turned away from Roosevelt's post-1939 foreign policy of actively engaging in the world and using American power to advance liberty and democracy. The election of 2006 deprived conservative Republicans—some critics said they were no longer Reagan Republicans—of control of Congress. And once again we are facing different problems, issues, and challenges from those Reagan faced during his years in office.

TRENCH-WARFARE AND OPEN-FIELD POLITICS

To understand the role of the Reagan legacy in our politics today, we need to understand the political era from which we have recently emerged and to appreciate the possibilities that now exist. But I think we can say one thing with considerable certainty: we have left a period of trench-warfare politics and have entered a period of open-field politics.

In the recent period of trench-warfare politics, the two parties, their politicians, and their voters were lined up like two armies in a culture war: two armies of approximately equal size, fighting it out over small pieces of disputed ground, striving to make the small gains that could make the difference between victory and defeat. We can see how closely matched the two armies were by looking at the numbers: Bill Clinton was reelected with 49 percent of the vote in 1996; Al Gore and George W. Bush were tied with 48 percent of the vote each in 2000; Bush beat John Kerry by a margin of 51 percent to 48 percent in 2004. In the five

House elections between 1996 and 2004, Republicans won between 49 percent and 51 percent of the popular vote, and Democrats won between 46 percent and 48.5 percent. This was an unusual degree of stability in voter preference, not seen since the 1880s. It started in the budget showdown between Bill Clinton and Newt Gingrich in the winter of 1995–1996 and ended sometime between Hurricane Katrina in August 2005 and the bombing of the Samarra mosque in February 2006. It was a period of great polarization, with political divisions centered on cultural and moral issues. Religion was the demographic factor that most highly correlated with voting behavior and, within each religious grouping, with the degree of religious observance.

Now we are in a different period, a period of open-field politics. The politicians and the voters are moving around. We saw this in the Democratic victory in the congressional elections of November 2006. This was a rejection of the Bush administration but not necessarily a conclusive verdict: voters knew they could install a Congress that would check George W. Bush without installing a wholly Democratic government. It was a vote on competence, not ideology; a rejection of the pork barrel politics and heavy spending that the Republican leadership used to hold onto its narrow congressional majority, not an embrace of Democratic policies. We have seen since then that the ratings of the Democratic Congress have plunged below even the low levels achieved by the Republican Congress.

In this period of open-field politics, we have seen changes in party identification, rather large changes in the context of American political history. In the 2004 exit polls, 37 percent of the voters identified themselves as Republicans and 37 percent as Democrats. In more recent polls, Democrats have had an advantage in party identification by as much as 10 percent—levels not seen since the 1970s. Some more recent polls, notably those taken by Scott Rasmussen, have seen a narrowing of the Democratic advantage in party identification, to levels about where they were during the period of trench-warfare politics. I think we may not have seen the last of these movements, and in either direction.

CHALLENGES TO THE REAGAN LEGACY

Is this a rejection of the conservative politics of Ronald Reagan? Not necessarily. That depends on how the voters respond to the policies and actions of the next president. This is not the first time we have had a period of open-field politics in the twenty years since Reagan left the White House. From 1990 to 1994, we were also in a period of open-field politics. At the beginning of the 1990s, political scientists said that the Republicans had a lock on the presidency and the Democrats had a lock on Congress, or at least on the House of Representatives. But they were wrong. In the next five years, we saw a series of unusual things. Bill Clinton was elected president, as George H. W. Bush's percentage of the vote declined by 17 percent—just about the same figure as for Herbert Hoover. The percentage for House incumbents of both parties declined in two successive elections, 1990 and 1992. The Republicans won the House for the first time in forty years in 1994 and won majorities in the Senate as well. Third-party candidates led in the polls—Ross Perot in spring 1992 and Colin Powell in fall 1995.

The net result of this was not a repudiation of Reagan conservatism. The Congress elected in 1994 and kept in office for twelve years had, as noted, more Reagan Republicans than any Congress during Reagan's presidency. Bill Clinton conceded that "the era of big government is over." That reaffirmation of something very much like Reagan conservatism was the result of voter reaction to the programs—notably Hillary Clinton's health care plan and Bill Clinton's tax increase—of the Clinton administration and the Democratic Congress. And it was reinforced by an electorate that remembered the 1970s, the failure of liberal policies symbolized by the gas lines of the 1970s and economic stagflation. The median-age voter in 1992 was born around 1947 and therefore came into adulthood at a time when he or she had to pay bills increased by inflation with paychecks eroded by bracket creep, and had to wait in line for an hour to buy gas.

In 2008 the median-age voter was born around 1963. This voter did not come into adulthood until the 1980s. He or she never waited in a gas line, never had to pay bills in a time of stagflation. This voter is more open to big government programs. This voter has lived in a time when we have had low-inflation economic growth more than 95 percent of the time. For this voter, that is the default mode of our economy, and any mild disturbance—rising gas prices, subprime mortgage defaults—is seen as an economic catastrophe. The economy, we are told, is the biggest issue on the voter's mind today. But it is an issue that neither party has satisfactorily addressed.

I would summarize the Reagan legacy in just a few words: markets work, morals matter, America must be strong in the world. That legacy is at risk, but it has not been rejected.

In this period of open-field politics, it may not be surprising that every presidential candidate's strategy for winning his or her party's nomination failed.

Mitt Romney's big-time buys failed to buy wins in Iowa and New Hampshire. Mike Huckabee failed to extend his appeal beyond evangelical and born-again Christians. Rudy Giuliani's failure to compete in the first six states sank him in the seventh. Fred Thompson ran stronger in the six months he was a noncandidate than in the four months he was a candidate.

John McCain was lucky in that his strategy failed first, at the end of June 2008. That meant his new strategy depended almost entirely on events outside his control, and lo and behold, they happened. Huckabee beat Romney in Iowa; Giuliani withdrew from New Hampshire; Thompson siphoned off votes from Huckabee in South Carolina; and Giuliani's collapse gave McCain the Cuban vote, which amounted to half his popular vote plurality in Florida.

As for the Democrats, Hillary Clinton's strategy was to win Iowa and New Hampshire and end the race early and cleanly. She lost in Iowa and came a few tears away from losing in New Hampshire. Barack Obama's strategy was to inspire people with an appeal that extended beyond racial and party lines. He brought new voters into the primaries and caucuses, even though the Clintons had some success in painting him as a Jesse Jackson–like candidate appealing to blacks only. John Edwards's 2008 populist strategy turned out to be less successful than his unsuccessful 2004 centrist strategy.

In our period of trench-warfare politics, the demographic factor most highly correlated with voting behavior—religion, or degree of religious observance—produced the map of red and blue states, red and blue counties, that is so familiar to us all. Voters now divide along different lines. States that were safe Republican or safe Democratic came into play; states that were closely divided leaned strongly to one party or the other. This is exactly what happened in the last period of open-field politics: the older George Bush won Florida and New Hampshire with 61 percent of the vote in 1988; in 1992 Clinton carried New Hampshire, and in 1996 he carried New Hampshire and Florida.

Those who are concerned that Reagan's legacy may be rejected should remember that his presidency was itself the product of a period of open-field politics. It was produced by a politician who kept principle firmly in mind while navigating turbulent political waters. It was a time when the old political rules were no longer operative—notably the rule that a Republican as conservative as Reagan could not win—and when the old political map was obsolete. During most of the 1980 cycle, his victory was seen as unlikely by most political pundits, and a prediction that he would carry forty-four of the fifty states would have been seen as preposterous. Yet he persevered in his principles and explained his policies in comprehensible language and made compelling arguments for them. That formula for success still exists.

CONTRIBUTORS

MICHAEL BARONE, senior writer for *U.S. News and World Report* and Fox News political analyst, includes the following among his books: *The Almanac of American Politics, The New Americans, Our Country, Hard America, Soft America,* and *Our First Revolution.*

ANDREW E. BUSCH, professor of government at Claremont McKenna College, is the author of *Reagan's Victory: The Presidential Election of 1980 and The Rise of the Right, Ronald Reagan and the Politics of Freedom, The Constitution on the Campaign Trail: The Surprising Political Career of America's Founding Document, The Front-Loading Problem in Presidential Nominations, Red over Blue: The Election of 2004,* and *The Perfect Tie: The True Story of the 2000 Presidential Election.*

JAMES W. CEASER, professor of politics at the University of Virginia, has authored *Presidential Selection, Reconstructing America, Liberal Democracy and Political Science, Reforming the Reforms,* and *Nature and History in American Political Development.* He has held visiting professorships at many European and American universities.

CHARLES W. DUNN is dean of the Robertson School of Government at Regent University. He is the author or editor of sixteen books, including *The Seven Laws of Presidential Leadership, The Future of Conservatism: Conflict and Consensus in the Post-Reagan Era,* and *The Future of Religion in American Politics.*

STEVEN F. HAYWARD, who serves as the F. K. Weyerhaeuser Fellow at the American Enterprise Institute, has written *The Age of Reagan: The Fall of the Old Liberal Order, 1964–1980, Greatness: Reagan, Churchill, and the Making of Extraordinary Leaders, Churchill on Leadership: Executive Success in the Face of Adversity,* and *The Real Jimmy Carter.* He is the coauthor of the annual *Index of Leading Environmental Indicators* and writes AEI's *Environmental Policy Outlook.*

HUGH HECLO, the Clarence J. Robinson Professor of Public Affairs at George Mason University, includes among his books *A Government of Strangers, Christianity and American Democracy,* and *Thinking Institutionally.* He is an elected member of the American Academy of Arts and Sciences and the National Academy of Public Administration, a Guggenheim Fellow, a Brookings Institution Senior Fellow, and the chair of the Ford Foundation research advisory committee, which published *The Common Good: Social Welfare and the American Future.* The American Political Science Association awarded him the John Gaus Award for lifetime achievement in 2002.

PAUL G. KENGOR, executive director of the Center for Vision and Values and professor of political science at Grove City College, has authored *God and Ronald Reagan, God and George W. Bush, The Crusader: Ronald Reagan and the Fall of Communism, The Judge: William P. Clark, Ronald Reagan's Top Hand,* and *Wreath Layer or Policy Player: The Vice President's Role in Foreign Policy.*

STEPHEN F. KNOTT, associate professor of political science at the U.S. Naval War College, is the author of *The Reagan Years, Alexander Hamilton and the Persistence of Myth, Secret and Sanctioned: Covert Operations and the American Presidency,* and *At Reagan's Side: An Oral History of the Man and the President.*

GEORGE H. NASH, Senior Fellow at the Russell Kirk Center for Cultural Renewal, is the author of *The Conservative Intellectual Movement in America since 1945* and a definitive, three-volume scholarly biography, *The Life of Herbert Hoover.* George Nash has lectured at the Library of Congress, the National Archives, the John F. Kennedy and Herbert Hoover presidential libraries, and the Gerald R. Ford Presidential Museum. His articles have appeared in the *National Review,* the *Wall Street Journal,* and the *New York Times Book Review.* Currently he serves as president of the Philadelphia Society.

INDEX